Speech to the Youth of Spain

# Speech to the Youth of Spain

BY RAMIRO LEDESMA RAMOS

Translated by Artemios Sylvanus

ANTELOPE HILL PUBLISHING

# CONTENTS

Preface........................................................................................ 1

I What Is Right in Front of Our Eyes? ............................... 5

   1. Sterility of Criticism ................................................... 5

   2. Historical Distance................................................... 7

   3. The Hour of the Empire and the Hour of Defeat ............... 8

   4. The Fruitless Conflict of the Nineteenth Century ........... 12

   5. The Restoration ....................................................... 14

   6. The Republic: April 14th ........................................... 17

II The Problems of National Youth ................................... 23

   1. Youth and the National Dimension........................... 24

   2. We Must Be Soldiers ................................................. 25

   3. The Unity of Spain................................................... 26

   4. A National Morality ................................................. 31

   5. Social Nationalism and National Socialism ............... 33

   6. Demographic Growth and Military Strength ............... 39

   7. The Pathways to International Strengthening............... 43

III Strategic Schemes.................................................... 47

  1. Political Action................................................... 47

  2. Direct Action..................................................... 49

  3. The Ruling Minority, the Political Power
  Spain Needs........................................................... 51

  4. The Issue Does Not Lie with Majorities............... 53

  5. The Reality of the Spanish People........................ 54

  6. The Catholic Church and Its Interference with the
  National Revolution................................................. 55

  7. The Contribution of the Workers, the Spanish
  Working Class......................................................... 58

IV Final Call to the Youth............................................ 61

  First Digression on the Revolutionary Sign of the Youths 62

    1. The Presence of the Youth................................. 62

    2. Conservative Eras and Revolutionary Eras........... 63

    3. The Messianic Consciousness of the Youth............ 65

    4. Facing Subversive Juncture................................ 66

    5. The Lack of Solidarity Among Youth................... 67

    6. Neither Moral Crisis, Nor Corruption, Nor
    Adventurism......................................................... 69

    7. The Rupture of "Progress"................................. 71

  Second Digression on the Current Profile of Europe.......... 72

    1. Pacifism, the League of Nations, and French
    Imperialism.......................................................... 73

      The Two Pacifisms.............................................. 73

      Geneva, A Reactionary Trench.............................. 74

      Geneva: Metropolitan Capital of French Imperialism
      ......................................................................... 75

Integral Pacifism: A Weary Attitude.................................76

2. Russian Bolshevism and the Global Projection of
Red Subversion ..............................................................78

Bolshevism, Russian National Revolution ...................78

The Global Bolshevik Revolution: A Failed Banner....80

3. Italian Fascism: The Second Message of Subversive
Youths...............................................................................82

Fascism and Marxism, Face to Face................................82

Fascism: A Revolutionary Phenomenon........................83

The Economic Interests of the Masses ..........................86

The Strengthening of the State Through the Inclusion
of Workers.........................................................................87

Fascism and the Democratic Bourgeois Institutions.88

4. Socialist Racism in Germany.............................................90

What Is the "National"?.....................................................90

The National Socialist Synthesis ...................................91

Not a Socialism for Man, but for the German...............93

In Service of Subversion ..................................................94

After the Marxist Wall, the Other Two: The Military
Oligarchy and the Junkers ..............................................95

5. The Impotence or Revolutionary Incapacity of
Marxism ..........................................................................97

The Triumph of Bolshevism in Russia..........................98

The Slogan of Class Exclusivity: The Dictatorship
of the Proletariat.............................................................100

Its Ignorance of the National .......................................102

Marxism Underestimates Revolutionary Values
of Maximum Effectiveness............................................102

6. The Demolition of Liberalism. Decrepitude of the Political and Economic Forms of the Individualistic Bourgeoisie ................................................................104

Its Individualistic Attitude .............................................105

Diminishment of Man.........................................................107

The Discontented Vanguard............................................108

Exhaustion and Contemplation of One's Own Ruins
................................................................................................109

7. Forced Unemployment. Humanity Exposed to the Elements..................................................................................110

The Ideal of Progressive Enrichment............................111

Man Reclaims His "Social" Sense....................................115

Unemployment: A Decisive Symptom............................116

8. The Uniformity of the Masses: The Political Uniform and its Authenticity.......................................................119

The Meaning of Uniformity.............................................119

The Emergence of the Masses .........................................121

The Political Uniform .......................................................123

Conclusion.............................................................................127

# PREFACE

Do you have a political book in your hands? Politics, in the only profound sense it possesses, is not an abstract science that feeds and sustains itself on general ideas and pure reasoning. Furthermore, it is not a science, nor does it really have much to do with science. Politics—and stating this does not imply any original invention—is an art, and above all, a strategy.

Therefore, if a book aspires to be in any way a political book, it has to address or tackle strategic challenges. It must be based on facts and, to a greater or lesser extent, extract from them the path toward new facts. There is no abstract politics. There is also no such thing as stagnant politics, politics at rest, the aims of which are fulfilled or accomplished in ten years.

Now it turns out that I have worked on this book during a few weeks in which I was forced to take on something of a pause, a vacation, from my tasks of active, concrete, and daily politics that, up until now, have been my work since 1931. During those years, I had the fortune of making a discovery, the importance and fertility of which a broad sector of the Spanish youth is already fully aware of.

That discovery was none other than finding a historical and political perspective for Spain that drew simultaneously from the only two truly effective triggers to make Spain what this generation must make it out to be: a just, great, and liberating fatherland.

Here are those two triggers: one, the national idea, the Fatherland as a historical enterprise and as a guarantee of the historical existence of all Spaniards; the other, the social idea, the socialist economy, as a guarantee of bread and economic well-being for the entire people. It seems the task of unifying these two banners has fallen to me, providing them with the necessary evocative symbols, and pointing out and laying the foundation of an organization that would interpret them. These elements are already there, moving around Spain. I believe they are inescapable and visible. They are the J.O.N.S.[1]

Well, this book has been written during the few weeks that I have remained outside the movement, due to irresolvable differences with those who currently hold sway within it. Therefore, it is the product of a time somewhat removed from active politics.

From there, its peculiar character, a character of discourse, not directed toward specific individuals in front of me, but toward the youth of Spain as a generic category, which is not easily put in line by anyone. Therefore, it is a discourse that must find its expression not in a direct style, as is typical of political speeches, but rather in a truly discursive and general manner. This prevents it from having a close projection on daily events and inevitably gives it an air of greater ambition.

Perhaps it is that certain things still need to be said in Spain in this way, with a certain conceptual framework and without the responsibility of political decisions that, when considered, will sooner or later become obligatory. It is appro-

---

[1] This is the Juntas de Ofensiva Nacional-Sindicalista ("Councils of National Syndicalist Offensive"), a nationalist and Fascist movement in Spain from the 1930s.

priate to do so, taking advantage of the circumstances in which, as I mentioned earlier, I find myself while writing these lines: outside the concrete discipline of a party.

I firmly believe that the entire world, and more specifically Europe, is currently going through a period of broad and significant transformations. In the final breakdown, which I publish at the end of this discourse, I maintain the view that the subversive realities that now govern the European transmutation are taking place under an unusual sign: that those executing and realizing them are not the traditionally revolutionary forces—such as Marxism, for example, which has come to our era equipped with revolutionary doctrine and tactics—but rather, others that have emerged in these recent years. These forces are characterized both by their national expression and their connection to youth, and they achieve their victory precisely at the expense of Marxism.

Therefore, this discourse, in light of the belief that the decisive manifestations of modern subversion are also approaching Spain, aims to exhibit to our youth the need for them to transform the revolution into a national revolution, liberating both the people and the Fatherland. It calls for seizing the transformative juncture as a great historical opportunity for Spain to fulfill its grand destinies. Whether this becomes a reality depends solely on the youth finding their path, rising to its challenges, and pursuing it militantly.

The very moment I have finished writing this book coincides with my reintegration into militant politics: a role that I acknowledge and see as fatally tied to my destiny.[2] I do not want to be among those who shy away from even the slightest part of its presence in the historical phase our Spanish fatherland is currently entering. I joined in battle again, pursuing the justice that the popular masses desire and need, and striving for the unity, greatness, and freedom of Spain.

---

[2] This is a prescient and poignant observation by the author, as he was executed in 1936 by the Republican militia, along with other presumed enemies of the Second Spanish Republic.

I only hope that these pages, born out of the interim period I mentioned earlier, serve to effectively guide the revolutionary struggles being carried out by the national youth.

# I

# WHAT IS RIGHT IN FRONT OF OUR EYES?

It seems, comrades, that all the omens today firmly point to the current Spanish youth as the only creative and liberating force that the Fatherland has at its disposal.

I believe this without hesitation; thus I say it to you with the zeal of camaraderie, the optimism of a soldier, and the hope inherent in every genuine and true Spaniard. This discourse aims to closely examine the experiences of the youth, revealing their current reality and the challenges they face. Ultimately, it seeks to outline the glorious destiny that their struggles should aspire to achieve.

## 1. Sterility of Criticism

The one thing that cannot be demanded of the current youth of Spain is to engage in a purely critical work. The fertility of criticism is always very limited. It is reduced to examining things from different angles, discovering their setbacks, their layers, their hidden truths and complexities. However, criticism alone will never allow one to completely disengage from what lies before them, nor will it ever be able to overcome and replace it with something entirely new and different.

If the youths are discontented with what they come across, they have no need to justify their attitude with a plethora of reasons. They do not need to explain their dissatisfaction, a task that would consume their entire youth and render them incapable of their own active and creative mission. Criticism is made according to certain standards, to patterns of perfection, and all of this, in reality, must be learned; thus it must be taught to the youth, for it is not inherent to them, nor does it form a part of them.

But a minimum level of criticism, in terms of appreciation or assessment of what lies ahead, is perhaps indispensable. In order to fulfill this minimal orientation, in the shortest number of pages possible, we will briefly cast our gaze upon the past of the Fatherland, and then, with a bit more focus, examine the period that immediately preceded us—the Restoration—in order to also scrutinize the ground we currently tread upon—the Republic.

Before we proceed, comrades, it is necessary to provide a warning, serving as both illustration and guide throughout this discourse: it appears since ancient times that Spain is fated to go through hardships. Spaniards have been aware of this from the moment they came into the world. Countless interpretations and explanations exist concerning the reasons why Spain has endured a history marked by struggles, difficulties, sorrow, and a lack of glory. It is time to abandon these preconceptions. They are false, dangerous, and serve no purpose whatsoever. Let it suffice to know that Spain is not burdened by any curse, and that Spaniards are neither incapable nor mediocre people. We are not constrained; there exist no boundaries or chains of any kind that prevent us from once again embedding Spain in universal history. The effort of a generation is all that is needed for this endeavor. Fifteen or twenty years will prove sufficient.

## 2. *Historical Distance*

It seems that Spain has been trying for two hundred or more years to find the most efficient way to die, and the limited historical knowledge possessed by the youth is sufficient to lead them to suspect that throughout this extensive period—whether it be a period of decadence or whatever else—Spain has been led and governed by people, groups, and ideas characterized by a mentality of dissolution, inheritance, and cowardice. To find complete victories and firm pulses, one must make the effort to journey far back along the path of history. We choose not to excessively dwell on that path. For just as it is enough for us to have a hunch or suspicion of the existence of that long and endless historical zone of liquidation in order to adopt an attitude of detachment toward it, it is also enough for us to suspect that our own race has indeed experienced magnificent days, in order to embrace an attitude of admiration and pride.

Apart from the fact that we should not wage our battle in the historical past, for our battle to be effective, we need close and real enemies. Thus, instead of looking back in search of a fateful event, a specific man at fault, or virulent ideas to blame for the deficient state of our Fatherland today, it is in our interest to perceive and uncover the facts, the individuals, and the ideas of this modern time. Otherwise, we run the risk of fighting against ghosts and illusory enemies, which would turn us into ghosts and repugnant deserters ourselves.

It is not permissible for us, then, to turn our gaze upon the Spanish past with any sense of languish, to rest in it and admire the greatness it possesses, which we lack today. If the glorious past of Spain served only that purpose, then we would have to renounce it without hesitation and erase it from the memory of Spaniards. However, Spain's past contains not only triumphant moments and magnificent successes, but also significant catastrophes and cacophonies. It is equally perilous to spend one's life solely celebrating the former and lamenting the latter.

The history of our Fatherland is a straightforward matter for us: we take responsibility for it and accept it in its entirety. However, for the purpose of the present, historical tradition holds limited relevance. Only the living values that reach us, whether they be good or bad, and thrive to inspire us, are deserving of our esteem. To answer the question of what history offers us, we need not delve deeply into chronicles and books. Instead, we must firmly focus our gaze on our own time, for it is within this context that we will find the information to form our response.

However, the historical dimension is fortunately unavoidable. To be aware of being born in the heart of a great nation, where individuals of the same heritage, endowed with similar capabilities, have accomplished remarkable historical feats, is undeniably a source of great inspiration and potential. It instills the certainty of pursuing legitimate ambitions, where reclaiming the reins of triumph is merely a matter of ingenuity, heroism, and willpower.

### 3. The Hour of the Empire and the Hour of Defeat

In the mid-sixteenth century, Spain reached its pinnacle. It was reaping the benefits of having achieved its national unity. It had discovered and largely conquered America. It possessed the most efficient institutions of the time. It had a colossal task, formulated by combining the two most powerful forces in history: religious faith and the Empire. Spain discovered and conquered territories with the cross in hand, winning them over for the Catholic faith. This faith played a pivotal role in consolidating the conquests and imbuing the new subjects with a deep sense of belief, effectively nationalizing them.

The spectacle that Spain presents from 1492 to 1588 is of a greatness rarely achieved by any people in any era. Our soil witnessed an authentic revolution, enabling the transition from a fragmented society with regional divisions, as seen during the Reconquista, to a nation driven by universal aspirations characterized by exploration, colonization, and ambition. The Empire of Charles V, with immense effort, facilitated this profound transformation. The arrival of a young king, with ties to the traditional Castilian dynasty, yet possessing distinct foreign attributes, was instrumental in shaping the Spanish people into assuming the imperial and powerful profile demanded by the times.

Emerging as a reactionary manifestation, the Spanish *comuneros* had various grievances to support their cause.[3] However, they stood in opposition to the truly revolutionary and magnificent phenomenon of the Empire. Their triumph, despite enduring humiliation and pain, was marked by episodes reminiscent of the rapacity of Caesar's early companions and a longing for past liberties. However, such resilience and sacrifice are the demands and requirements history places upon those entrusted with the role of catalysts, leaders, and global creators. If the *comuneros* had triumphed in Villalar and imposed a "national" and narrow reign upon Charles V, the grandeur of the sixteenth century in Spain might have been thwarted. The endeavors of the conquistadors might not have come to fruition, and, of course, Spain's victorious projection onto Europe would not have existed. The conflict between the *comuneros* and the imperial conception of Charles V represents perhaps the first significant event in our homeland that reveals a deep divide, a rupture not easily reconcilable, between two factions of Spain regarding the differing understanding of the historical destiny of the Spanish people.

---

[3] Between 1520 and 1521, the Guerra de las Comunidades de Castilla (War of the Communities of Castile), or as it is better known in English, The Revolt of the Comuneros occurred..

Just as Spain's ascent was great, triumphant, and swift, so its subsequent descent was equally steep. However, it should not be misunderstood that this decline spanned an extended period of decadence. No, the decline originated from the ruling institutions—the monarchy and the Church—at the beginning of the seventeenth century, permeating the spirit and psyche of the people. From that point onward and up to the present, Spain has not experienced a proper decline, but rather an absence, a real departure from history.

And perhaps it should be said, comrades, that the term "decline" is not even fitting for Spain's hour of descent. When speaking of a nation in decline, it implies that such a decline occurs due to internal causes, originating from the nation itself, as a sort of natural phenomenon of aging. We must resist accepting this judgment regarding what is commonly referred to as Spain's decline. Our Fatherland—and far from concealing this fact, I believe, on the contrary, it is important to reiterate it often—*was defeated*. In the history of Spain from the seventeenth century onward, it is not difficult to comprehend: *Spain was defeated, overcome by rival empires.* These empires bore a dual nature. One was economic, commercial, and material—represented by England. The other was moral, spiritual, and cultural—embodied by the Reformation. But would anyone dare to take the criminal stance of siding with the victors?

For whatever reason, Spain could not find a way to capture the complementary empire that had been its strength and glory during the sixteenth century. That complementary empire, had it not been possessed, and which would inevitably have fallen into the hands of others, was to be the driving force behind the economic revolution that was already foreseen. Spain missed the chance to be the pioneering nation of the new commercial, bourgeois, and capitalist economy, and this displacement also deprived it of dominance, leaving it without a nourishing foundation, without a future.

Well, certain instruments are not wielded with impunity, and what led Spain to defeat was its almost exclusive attachment to values of an extra-material and even extra-historical nature. Since the significant reform of the Church carried out by the Catholic monarchs, Spain, as a powerful entity, has utilized religious faith as one of its most potent instruments. Spain paid a high price for the services lent by Catholicism to its empire. Thanks to Spain, to the collective genius of Spain, evident and effective both in the Council of Trent with its theologians and on the battlefields under the banner of the Catholic cross, Catholicism survived in the West, while in Rome, it awaits a new opportunity to aspire to the spiritual unity of the world. Without Spain, without its sixteenth century, Catholicism might have been engulfed, and the religious life of Europe would have been represented in its totality by a collection of more or less Christian national factions.

Spain, I repeat, was defeated. The distinction lies in the fact that one can only be considered defeated after having fought; understanding this nuance sets apart the defeated from the deserters and the cowards. After its historical defeat, Spain had not much else to do in the world but wait. It lived in liquidation, as the culminating era also provided great spiritual and territorial wealth, which served wonderfully for generations of heirs and squanderers. Little by little, the territorial empire naturally disintegrated, and the nation returned to its humble domestic life, distant from the great conflicts that continued to unfold in the world. The people remained in their place, loyal to their nationality, which they defended during the Wars of Independence against the most powerful armies in Europe.[4] However, they lived with a sense of disillusionment, hoping that their last meager resources would be well managed. The liquidation process proceeded without any disruptions from revolutions. The institutions persisted throughout the two centuries of depression, and their most significant accomplishment was preserving the

---

[4] This refers to the Spanish American Wars of Independence.

integrity of the Iberian Peninsula—not without dangers, though. At the beginning of the seventeenth century, a plan to disintegrate and balkanize the peninsular territory was already circulating in Europe, with Europe pulling at Catalonia. There were even French viceroys appointed there. Nevertheless, that cancerous process was overcome, and the unity of Spain was preserved. It has been the only victory since the zenith of the Empire, even though its stature dimmed in the West due to the non-assimilation of Portugal and its humiliation in the south with Gibraltar in the hands of England.

### 4. The Fruitless Conflict of the Nineteenth Century

Throughout the nineteenth century, a double drama of conflicting forces unfolded: one of these forces, attempting to resurrect and defend Spain's tradition, disregarded its antecedent, the Empire; the other was intent on the liberation from those traditions. The former could not genuinely restore the ancient Spanish tradition, nor could the latter succeed in bringing about any kind of revolution.

During the nineteenth century, the Spaniards became polarized around these two unyielding formulas, defended with such determination and tenacity that both have survived a hundred years of mutual struggles, with neither side surrendering, nor achieving complete victory in their endeavors.

The first thing that should be observed in the political struggles of the nineteenth century is that they were not properly political, but rather religious conflicts. If one contemplates it from a distance, it displays an irredeemable sterility. The defenders of tradition could only offer Spain the prospect of preserving its Spanish reserve, so to speak, while the pseudo-revolutionaries could have played a truly positive historical role if their triumph had led to the introduction of new possibilities offered to the world by technical culture, industrial mechanization, and the vigorous nationalism corresponding to a numerous and wealthy bourgeoisie.

They were, I repeat, religious struggles, though they were put in motion in the political arena, not between two entirely different religions, as one would assume, but between those who were Catholic—although, of course, the Spanish had always been Catholic, through the state and by means of the state—and those who were not Catholic or only lukewarmly Catholic. Therefore, the conflict unfolded around the clergy rather than around the doctrines. On one end the clerics, on the other, the anti-clerics.

The two factions that fought throughout the entire century were unable to obtain the full effects of their victories. Traditional, Catholic Spain, gathered around the churches, could not aspire to more than just a static attitude of preservation and defense. Others, more detached in the way they operated in a country with inward-facing economic forms, entangled themselves in a series of obscure doctrinal issues that bordered on national betrayal and failed to gain the collaboration of the masses. As a consequence of the incapacity of both sides, the only constant thread became the never-ending series of military pronouncements, turning the army, more than an organization for warfare, into a breeding ground for politicians and statesmen: Espartero, O'Donnell, Narváez, Serrano, Prim, and so on.

Spain urgently needed a period in which the two nineteenth-century banners would disappear, much like the Guadiana River, into an underground course. After the failure of both—after traditional and Catholic Spain did not triumphantly secure its fanaticism in the Palace of Madrid in the ideal form of a warrior and missionary, of expansion and strength—thus dissatisfied, Spain declared itself incapable of raising a national, violent, and Jacobin-like ideal upon which to build a new society and new institutions; both tendencies equally deserved to be dismantled and expelled from the realm of political possibilities. However, those intentions were hardly begun. Both also lacked strong national sentiments. For some, tradition and patriotism consisted of defending privileges, religious claims, and local and familial ways of life, in other words, they were always parts, factions. For the others, the revolution was linked to the freedom to imitate, to the predatory pull of the cities against the countryside, and so forth. Let us recognize a fertile value in nineteenth-century Spanish liberalism: its sense of Spain's unity.

## 5. The Restoration

All of this came crashing down during the Restoration.[5] This regime was purely a consequence of the double failure that Spain experienced throughout the long and turbulent circumstances that have been referenced. The Restoration had a clear and historical mission: to submerge the two sterile currents whose failure had just been witnessed, and to put Spain in a position to produce a new national ideal, drawn naturally from its own genius and supported by social forms different from those that had sustained the old struggles. To achieve this, it would have to live on the fringes of national life, neither supporting nor opposing it.

The Restoration began with a paradox. As it so happened, this resulted in the constitutional monarchy; the validity of the Constitution known as "'76" would become an effective and fruitful period in which it managed to sustain itself without appealing to the reality of the national situation.[6] It was considered evident at that time that this reality was disastrous. This was the moment that the politician Cánovas, the chief builder and guide of the Restoration, embarked on the

---

[5] The Restoration, or the Bourbon Restoration, is the period beginning on 1874, after a military coup ended the First Spanish Republic and restored the monarchy, and ending in 1931, with the inception of the Second Spanish Republic.

[6] The Constitution of 1876 was written during the Restoration period, and was enforced throughout.

task equipped with the two most suitable ingredients for the work ahead: radical skepticism and a keen sense of statecraft.[7]

The Restoration indeed succeeded in one of its purposes: to persist. It lasted for fifty years. Half a century is a sufficient period of a time for a nation or a regime to experience the culmination of its triumph or the clamor of its failure.

The reign of Alfonso XIII—by the king's notorious and personal will—was a continuous struggle to provide the constitutional monarchy with a solid foundation. That struggle materialized in its military policy, empowering the officer corps with a certain cognizance of, and enthusiasm for, the unity of Spain and its grandiosity; it also appeared in the Moroccan expansion, as a potential ground where some national optimism could flourish.[8] In Maura's pursuit to substitute the anomalous and *cacique*-based support of the state with genuine endorsement from what he called the citizenry, the king engaged in a continuous struggle for a solid foundation.[9] Furthermore, efforts were made to accelerate the country's industrialization, diversifying the economy beyond its sole reliance on agrarian and landlord support of the regime.

Outside and against the state, the ideas and groups operating under a revolutionary banner set up their tents quite simply: they gathered the ideological remnants of their nineteenth-century predecessors, critically scrutinized Spain's entire intellectual life, weakened the emerging military spirit, fostered disintegrative and autonomist tendencies, embraced

---

[7] Antonio Cánovas del Castillo served six terms as the Spanish prime minister, and was largely responsible for designing and bringing to power the government that followed with the restoration of Bourbon rule. He was killed by an anarchist.

[8] Alfonso XIII oversaw the Rif War (1921–1926), in which Spanish colonialists fought Berber tribes for control over northern Morocco. This conflict was controversial, with some seeing it as necessary to preserve Spanish rule in Africa, and others seeing it as a waste of Spanish lives and resources.

[9] Antonio Maura Montaner was the Spanish prime minister during the largely unpopular reign of Alfonso XIII. They would become politically estranged. Maura was opposed to *caciquismo*, a political system dominated by local political bosses.

complete defeatism regarding Morocco, and maintained a certain lukewarmness and ignorance toward any national idea or sense of patriotism.

In addition, labor organizations emerged, expanding at the same pace as industrialization, naturally adopting a class-conscious approach and a doctrine consistent with all the practical aspects mentioned earlier.

In 1923, the last year of the constitutional rule during the Restoration, Spain encountered two significant failures. First was the state and the regime, which continued without having expanded its foundation of support in the slightest; the other was of the opposing forces hostile to the state, who had also failed to provide what was truly needed: a unified national front, with genuine concern for the historical destiny of the Spanish fatherland and the immediate daily interests of the entire population. Salvation could have been found there, especially if they had the intrepidity to audaciously camp within the very heart of the regime, with the ambivalent purpose of either causing its collapse if it succumbed to its own decay, or using and preserving it patriotically if its continuity was deemed valuable.

Since the remedy did not come from outside, the king extracted it from within the state: he turned to the army. Thus begins the military dictatorship of Primo de Rivera, the fundamental flaw of which lay in the fact that it did not arise from or stem from a national reality.[10] In a certain way, it continued the essence of the Restoration, seeking to provide Spain with a new historical margin, hoping that it would recover its consciousness as a united, ambitious, and promising nation.

But with the dictatorship, the state set course toward the path of resolutions, toward decisive moments. If the dictatorship failed to genuinely strengthen and solidify the official

---

[10] Miguel Primo de Rivera y Orbaneja, 2nd Marquis of Estella, GE, began a military coup in September 1923 as a result of political crises, which occurred as a response to the Rif War.

directions of the regime, it would inevitably collapse, even if there was nothing respectable or profound rising against it.

The military dictatorship accelerated Spain's material and industrial progress. It achieved almost unanimous support from the country, especially among those with mature, sensible, and conservative views. A noteworthy success was also enjoyed in Morocco. This dictatorship lasted almost seven years before dying, exhausted, succumbing naturally to old age. The dictatorship died of old age just at seven years, much like the preceding constitutional period perished at fifty after its inception.

Primo de Rivera provided Spain with seven years of uninterrupted peace, during which a genuine economic boom took place. However, he did not initiate any agrarian reforms—agricultural property still remained the main pillar of the regime—and he never succeeded in securing the collaboration of the youth, despite the dictatorship coinciding with the emergence of an active youth consciousness in Spain. This youth consciousness needed to be safeguarded from divisive, antinational, and negative influences.

The military dictatorship was replaced by General Berenguer's government, which aimed to restore the old constitutional and orthodox form of the Restoration.[11] However, this attempt failed swiftly and irreparably. It served as a catalyst for the rapid organization, in a liberal, propitious, and mild atmosphere, of the fall of the monarchial regime and its substitution by the Republic.

## 6. The Republic: April 14th

The phenomenon of April 14th, 1931, the proclamation of the Republic, inaugurates the current situation in which we

---

[11] This is Dámaso Berenguer y Fusté, 1st Count of Xauen, the general and politician who served as the Spanish prime minister during the end of the reign of Alfonso XIII.

find ourselves today, the very reality in which the youth must now operate.[12] That is why it is of utmost importance that we properly understand its significance.

The teeming masses, the great electoral majorities that voted for the Republic, did not bring to power men, ideas, and a political reality that emerged cohesively, disciplined, and efficiently from their own ranks. Instead, they facilitated certain groups, ideas, and individuals who, at that moment, represented opposition to the old monarchical system of the Restoration and the dictatorship.

Indeed, on April 14th, 1931, power was handed over to that tearful, critical, and dissatisfied entourage that had been closely following the unfortunate and wavering steps of official and traditional Spain for a very long time. Recognizing this is of great importance because it signifies that the republican movement that gave life to the Constitution of 1931 was not a transcendence of past conflicts, nor did it represent the dawn of something national and new. Instead it was fueled almost entirely by an attitude already tested and familiar, belonging to the same political process as that of the Restoration.

The similarity between the events of the two dates, September 13th, 1923, and April 14th, 1931, is notable and striking. In both instances, the Spanish people failed to infuse them with their own distinctive character and remained passive observers. On September 13th, the Spanish people seemed to regard it as excellent that a general, or whoever it might be, took action on their behalf to rid the Restoration of its *cacique* gangs. Similarly, in 1931, instead of triumphantly embracing a movement of their own, an embodiment of a solemn historical moment like the collapse of the monarchy, they also acted from the sidelines and bestowed significant credit upon individuals, groups, and ideas that had been unsuccess-

---

[12] To be clear, this is the Second Spanish Republic.

fully vying for political consideration from the Spanish for over sixty years.

The only fertile ground of April 14th perhaps lies solely in permitting those individuals, groups, and ideas to depart from their traditional and incessantly critical stance to reveal and exhibit their support from positions of power. I assign them this mission, which is akin to finally exploring the dark side of the moon. Their victory, then, is within the old and traditional system. It was achieved by virtue of the same polemical style that can be easily recognized in the conflicts and controversies of the nineteenth century: a victory, ultimately of a revolving and cyclical nature.

April 14th, 1931, then, marks the end of a historical process, not the beginning of a new one. This is its essential characteristic, which explains its swift failure and renders that date incapable of serving as the starting point for the national revolution that Spain will inevitably undertake someday.

Indeed, the triumphant groups in April brought forth elements of such nature that one could expect anything but a national victory for Spain. Ah! If April 14th had taken place under the banner of "Long live Spain!" the revolutionary event would have been something different and would evidently have represented the inaugural date of the national revolution. But of course, it did not happen this way, and if we review the intentions of the various forces that gave life and reality to that date, we also find that it could not have happened this way. Not a single one of the several groups of April 14th acted with the purpose of turning the revolution into a national revolution. That was the deception, and that was ultimately also the divisive seed of the nascent Republic.

† † †

A national revolution on April 14th should have been the guarantee for Spain that everything the old monarchy no longer provided would become possible through it: an effective unification of the entire people, countering separatist tensions in Catalonia and the Basque Country. It would have swiftly established a strong and popular Spanish army, addressed the moral dispersion of the Spaniards, and unified them in the worship of the common homeland. It would have liberated the peasants and supported small farmers, introducing a bold plan for the development of electrical and steel industries, combating the country's depopulation with a demographic policy aiming to double Spain's current population. In response to unemployment and crisis, it would have nationalized transportation, boosted small distribution industries, and rapidly increased the purchasing power of the people. Moreover, it would have boldly pursued a vigorous and independent international policy, rejecting any subservience to France and England.

That would have been a national revolution, and yet contrary to that was the reality of April 14th, 1931.

The prospects of that date needed to be illusory; the intellectuals who gave it expression represented a traditional discrepancy with the historical significance of the institutions that owed their unity to their origins, arriving at the absurd belief that our entire history was a mistake. The disintegrating groups that influenced and sustained the emerging regime from the periphery of Spain naturally lacked a comprehensive and total concern for Spain. The Marxists were naturally detached from the problem. The old liberal-demolitionist parties, such as the Radical Party, represented weakness, compromise, and concession. So who, then, would infuse the April revolution with national content, and who would work within it to extract historical national consequences?

Therefore, April 14th was born crippled and incapacitated, incapable of yielding a national revitalization for Spain.

† † †

Now then, having acknowledged and accepted these limitations, did April 14th harbor fertile prospects for social coexistence among Spaniards? In other words, with any national path severed, any inclination for the revolution to make Spain first and foremost a strong and vigorous nation discarded, did it at least achieve a more agreeable social order for all Spaniards and enthusiastic acceptance from the workers and laborers? The answer leaves no room for doubt: not at all.

There were three popular insurrections—above all, October 6th, a terrible date, when not only the anarcho-syndicalist workers, who had been in disagreement with the regime from its inception, took up arms, but also the socialist workers, the direct architects and builders of the Constitution and all the institutions of the Republic.

April 14th meant nothing, neither for the national order, nor for the social order. Its own creators proclaimed their monstrous mistake on October 6th, 1934, the date of the Generalitat's insurrection and the Marxist subversion of Asturias.[13] October 6th has one and only one significance: the torpedoing and sinking of the pseudo-revolution of April by those who carried it out and illuminated it.

That, comrades, is the reality, and in correspondence with it, there is not much room for lamentation. Among these failed revolutionary possibilities, there is also the treason of a certain youthful spirit that manifested in Spain months before the Republic. This youth movement did not find any satisfaction. The young were not understood, and the April gov-

---

[13] On October 6th, 1934, a general strike and an uprising began in Catalonia, due to disagreements about conservatives in government. Catalonia declared independence from Spain, but military intervention forced its surrender the next day. By the Generalitat's insurrection, the author refers to the occupation of the Palau de la Generalitat, the government building, by Lluís Companys, the president of Catalonia.

ernment did nothing but corrupt those who appeared as leaders, including themselves in the bureaucratic payroll of their secretariats.

Here we find ourselves, comrades, and the reality of the regime, the latest one before us, which has emerged as a response to the subversions of October, is a fitting conclusion to the radical sterility of the system. Spain and the Republic now find themselves in the hands of the old, faded, and inoperative oligarchic groups, as one could imagine. The radical *cedista* government brought to the surface what April 14th truly carried within itself, along with its naive pseudo-revolutionary eruptions, which was a circling around the known and failed relics of nineteenth-century Spain, having become intertwined with them, and ultimately marking the end of an era, the culmination of political decadence: not a dawn, nor a beginning, nor a fruitful inauguration of anything.[14]

†     †     †

We summarize the panorama of the last hundred years: the failure of traditional Spain, the failure of subversive Spain (both in their struggles of the nineteenth century), the failure of the Restoration (constitutional monarchy), the failure of Primo de Rivera's military dictatorship, and the failure of the Republic. Let us see how on top of this great pyramid of failures, we can build a formidable, lasting, and resounding historical success. The slogan is: *national revolution!*

---

[14] A *cedista* is a supporter of the CEDA, or the Confederación Española de Derechas Autónomas (Spanish Confederation of Autonomous Rights), a conservative Catholic political party.

# II

# THE PROBLEMS OF NATIONAL YOUTH

Before such a panorama, the youth will find it difficult to establish a solid basis to hold onto. They are alone, and far from being a cause for concern and demotivation, this may just present a great opportunity that Spain needs. Desertion is out of the question, as it would lead to historical catastrophe, the first consequence of which would be the disappearance of Spain and the degradation and enslavement of its people.

The Spanish people have encountered a barrier, in the presence of a dividing line. To be unaware of this is equivalent to deceiving oneself, and to abandon the only feasible banner today: that of breaking down that barrier and crossing that line with determined steps.

Well, it just so happens that in Spain, there are sufficient forces and energies to emerge victorious from this historical trial and to shatter into a thousand pieces the long train of cancerous impediments. These forces and energies can only truly be effective if the national revolution includes them in its strategy, giving satisfaction to their just demands.

The exact problem of the Spanish youth at this moment is no more and no less than achieving a full awareness of their historical mission. They must also understand that if this mission is not accomplished or fulfilled, Spain will perish, and the Spanish people will be left spiritually and economically bereft.

## 1. Youth and the National Dimension

Indeed, if the youth examine their heritage today—which is to say, who they are and what they own—they will discover, in accordance with what is written, that it is quite limited and simple. Far from being an obstacle or hindrance to the tasks that lie ahead, this simplicity and limitedness position them at the very essence of their destiny.

Let us outline here what this limited heritage consists of and what it obliges. What does the Spanish young person really have up his sleeve?

First and foremost, he has his youth: a life projected into tomorrow, toward the future. He also possesses a national dimension: the profound, decisive, and formidable reality of being born Spanish, of being a Spaniard. This last part encompasses and affirms his human nature, defining and presenting his proof of humanity. For we are complete and fulfilled individuals to the extent that we are complete and fulfilled Spaniards, not conversely.

He has nothing else. He lacks wealth, wisdom, power, nor does he have individual destiny already achieved, and he has no political doctrine to serve. In short, he has nothing but those two values mentioned earlier. This is because he is present at a time in Spain when the current governing forces, both in politics and in social and economic matters, find themselves in a period of impotence, contradiction, and crisis.

Now then, it seems that the youth not only lack any normal possibility of development today, but they also face the very danger of having their own peculiar baggage, that which defines and burdens them, torpedoed and lost. In essence, their youth and their fundamental dimension of being Spaniards may be shattered and irreversibly lost.

If, at this stage, in these moments, Spain were to falter as an independent and free nation, the youth would be left amputated, impaired, and irreversibly reduced to mere remnants.

The fact that we find ourselves facing the final stages of a very long and secular process of decomposition places us on the edge of both the abyss and the Empire. However, Spain must and can be saved, and every day it becomes increasingly evident that the youth constitute its unique possibility of salvation.

Recognizing that the recent and immediate past of the Fatherland does not offer any firm ground for the youth, and that the distant and remote past, though magnificent and splendid, is ungraspable due to its own seclusion, the consequence of all this is that the youth are alone, with only those two things mentioned before.

And so, we must depart from that reality, accept it as it is, and organize the actions of the youth in consideration of it.

## 2. We Must Be Soldiers

The current Spanish youth are facing a stage similar to the one experienced by all peoples and races in their initial phase of expansion and growth. It is also a stage similar to that of those who know themselves as prisoners, surrounded by enemies.

First and foremost, under such circumstances *we must be soldiers*.

The youth of Spain now face this most demanding dilemma: either militarize or perish. Ignorance is not an option.

Now then, if the problem for the Spanish youth is indeed a military one, then they have the same challenge faced by all soldiers. The immediate task is to approach with precision and rigor the following three essential questions, essential to all armies:

a) How to equip oneself: which instruments should be chosen for their struggles.

b) How to move: what their strategy should be and what kind of alliances and support are suitable for them.

c) What goals to pursue: what the immediate and distant objectives are and what conquests they seek to achieve.

The solution, comrades—the precise and just resolution of these three sets of problems—is the victorious accomplishment of the national revolution, the fundamental and sole banner of the youth. Here, in a specific and brief manner, we address them, without forgetting the current reality in which we, the Spanish people, find ourselves.

It is undoubtedly convenient, for methodical purposes, to begin our inquiry with the third of the statements, which refers to the types of goals and the desires that we strive for. We are, then, at the heart of the reason behind the historical mobilization of the youth, the very justification for the national revolution that we claim they are meant to undertake.

It is evident that the essential conquests must be those without which Spain will inexorably head toward definitive historical ruin. These are the three or four indispensable consensuses, the very presence of which is crucial for Spain's survival and continuity.

Among those three or four unavoidable consensuses, which cannot be denied, naturally lies this one:

### 3. The Unity of Spain

If Spain is not something real for Spaniards, something whose essence is not open to questioning, then Spain does not exist as a fatherland. There is no fatherland if, within its boundaries, ideas and people contrary to its very existence are allowed to be openly present and public. For those elements are, by definition, characteristic of what is found outside, foreign, of the presumed enemy.

The unity of Spain is the oldest national unity established in Europe. Thanks to this historical advantage in the process of forming modern nationalities, Spain was the most cultured, strongest, and wealthiest nation in the world during the sixteenth century. While other European nations were struggling to create their unity and discovering their national components, Spain had already surpassed that initial stage and was on its way to becoming a potent empire.

Spanish national unity has indeed been the thing that has made our noble past possible. But we must remember: its mission is not only to explain and justify history, but also to exist as a basic pillar of today's Spain, as a primordial and fundamental element of the entire nation.

Evidently, the affirmation of unity is at the forefront of the revolutionary demands of the national youth. As long as the Constitution of 1931 remains in effect, as long as a large portion of Spaniards believe that the disintegrating process at the periphery is merely a dispute over the form the state should take, the national unity will be in permanent danger of defeat (and being in danger is, for many reasons, no way to exist). The autonomist eruptions of Catalonia and the Basque Country are part of the same path of liquidation and decomposition of Spain that followed the collapse of the Empire, from Rocroi to 1898.[15] It is no coincidence that those eruptions emerged as problematic phenomena after this last date, or in other words, once the overseas disintegration was closed and concluded, as if the historical cancer were ready to sink its teeth into the unity of the peninsular territories.

Spain possesses all the necessary historical credentials to maintain its unity. This was established in the fifteenth cen-

---

[15] Rocroi refers to the 1643 battle of Rocroi, a part of the Thirty Years' War, in which the seemingly invincible Spanish infantry was defeated by France. 1898 refers to the Spanish-American War, in which the United States defeated the Spanish and thereby became the predominant power in the Caribbean.

tury by the only powers that represented the political will of all Spaniards, giving satisfaction to not only the aspirations of their time, but also to the beautiful dream of unity cherished by all the Hispanics since Roman times.

Now then, what matters today is not precisely historical credentials. The struggle for unity is not fought between two groups of historians or jurists. Given that, for various reasons, the factions inclined toward the disintegrating thesis wield considerable influence, manipulating powerful political mechanisms, and having managed to gain a broad and dangerously influential following of moderates who compromise and make concessions, the problem rests entirely within the hands of this voluntarily decisive lever to which, in the end, peoples appeal to justify their historical existence.

Therefore, everything indicates that the struggle for unity bears the character of a struggle for the existence of Spain. We might be facing the necessity of Spain revalidating its credentials, much exactly like in 1808, though this time, those posing such grave questions are not foreigners, but wayward Spaniards, narrow-minded and bereft of spirit, unworthy of Spain's mission and the grandeur of its future.[16]

The current problem of unity requires a deliberate solution: a solution imposed by a firm will, expressed and fulfilled by those who earn the right to secure Spain's historical permanence. That is why, and only why, it is a revolutionary slogan and not an electoral agenda. Naturally, we do not believe, like Renan, that the nations are a continuous and permanent plebiscite; on the contrary, we believe that they have their roots beyond and within everyday things.[17] However, Spain,

---

[16] Here, 1808 may refer to the Spanish American Wars of Independence, mentioned above, or the overlapping Peninsular War, in which Spain, Portugal, and the United Kingdom united to fight the invading First French Empire during the Napoleonic Wars.

[17] The reference here is to Ernest Renan, a French scholar who in his lecture "What is a Nation?" came to the conclusion that the maintenance of nationhood is contingent on the desire of its members to remain a nation, in the fashion of their democratic consent to shared nationhood.

due to reasons beyond our control (meaning the newly arrived generations) is truly facing the question of its unity, its very existence. Therefore, we are confronted with the problem of resolving and conquering it.

And here is how the very intensification and aggravation of our national problem, that of being withered and absent for over two hundred years, will provide us with a certain opportunity for resurgence. The trajectory that follows the disintegrating forces is one that can only be overcome or halted through war, which is to say, through a revolution. Its first setback, on October 6th, was due to the intervention of cannons.

Unity cannot consist of a simple destruction of the separatist aspirations that currently thrive in Catalonia and the Basque Country, even if it must triumph violently over them. Spain must represent and be a living, active, and present reality for all Spaniards. It needs to be a profound moral force, a historical power that carries with it the optimistic spirit of the entire nation.

The unity of Spain presents itself to us today as the first and most valuable goal of the youth. We cannot be resigned to tolerating a unity in danger, deficient and incomplete, for a single moment. Without unity, we Spaniards will always lack a secure framework upon which we can seriously build anything. So, until true unification is achieved, until the forces that currently advocate for the weakening of national bonds are deprived of their roots, the Spanish people will continue to live their sad destiny as a defeated nation, lacking in historical dignity and genuine freedom.

The defense of a policy of concessions to regional factions that demand autonomy is equivalent to defending the historical process of Spanish decomposition. It is equivalent to being content with the worst aspects of our past, desiring our defeat to be permanent. It is equivalent to an attitude of shame and embarrassment for Spain, having once been an empire. It implies believing that Spain is a monstrous mistake of history;

thus, it is deemed magnificent to dismantle it stone by stone until the point of its absolute annihilation.

Sometimes one comes across disintegrators who invoke historical facts and reasons to support their thesis. It is not easy to determine if these facts and invocations hold any respectability from the perspective of historical truth. Naturally, one might be inclined to deny it, because history is made by the victorious powers, especially if those victories embody and solidify the very fertile spirit of history. Such is the case with Spain and its unity, ingeniously created in a clean, fertile, and effective manner. We find that this unity is not only a formidable historical achievement, which gives way to surprising accomplishments, but also an extremely relevant possession for us, the Spaniards of this era, and as essential as the air we breathe.

The defense of the unity of Spain cannot only be driven— although, in many cases, this is a sufficient reason—by the desire to prevent the nation from fragmenting and disappearing—in other words, dying—which is an anguishing spectacle for any patriot. Instead, it stems from a necessity on our part, the Spaniards of the present, something that, if we don't possess, reduces us to a despicable, inferior, and shameful human category. Thus, unity is not a conservative slogan, on the defensive, but a revolutionary slogan, a necessity for today and tomorrow.

Spain is not just any amorphous territory lacking history and a future. If it were, its cracking and disintegration would matter little. On the contrary, Spain today is one of the nations closest to achieving a global, economic, and political status to be envied. It is one of the nations with the possibility of reaching a splendid era, after a long wait, and crossing through miserable, harsh, and endless periods of decay and weakness.

In a moment like this, in an hour like this, placing persistent calls in favor of Spain's dispersion is not only an act of betrayal, but also an act of foolishness and lunacy. It is, without a doubt, a reactionary stance, in much the same sense, as mentioned before, to remain in a line of service to liquidating tradition, in reference to the national past, in the tradition of defeat.

## 4. A National Morality

Many of the vicissitudes our people have gone through are due to the inexistence or neglect of a national morality; Spaniards adopted the habit of not needing or missing it. Spaniards, especially in the last half-century, have lived without remembering at all what they were. They could aspire to be wise men, plutocrats, judges, even military officers, without recalling or giving much importance to their national condition, their condition as Spaniards.

This is a shameful fact that the youth must rise against. Do they not already suspect that without a national dimension, wisdom becomes pedantry, wealth becomes thievery, justice becomes a farce, and the military turns into pure adventurism?

There is a morality of the Spanish people that neither obliges nor serves those who are not part of it. Without this morality, we would achieve very little. Precisely, it is through the service of such a morality and its acceptance that the historical existence of great nations is nurtured. And during those periods when this morality is abandoned or derelict, people fall into degradation and slavery. Thus, their existence is shattered, their historical will to live is weakened, and such circumstances coincide with economic and political subordination to other nations.

Spain must anchor its unity and strength on the broad shoulders of a national morality that is optimistic and rigid. To be Spanish is not a disgrace, but a splendid gift of life: a gift in permanent danger and risk, which can only be retained and conserved by nurturing it every day with an ethic of sacrifice for the fatherland.

Service to Spain and sacrifice for Spain are moral values superior to any others, and their popular validity, their acceptance by "all of the people," is the only guarantee we Spaniards have to a morally profound existence. Ah, the great crime of not accepting this sacrifice, to deny and shun it! People without national morality are never free. They are either exploited and tyrannized by a minority from within their own country, also devoid of any moral anguish and commitment to the historical life of "all of the people," or they are under the deception and guise of independence by a foreign nation.

There is nothing to be done, comrades, if we fail to instill and circulate a national morality among the Spaniards. This moral asceticism is already within us all, and by its virtue, we desire to save our fellow compatriots politically, historically, and economically. It forms the basis of our action, and it is truly what elevates and distinguishes our military efforts from mere armed bands that others may create.

In the name of this morality and its obligations, we carry out a revolutionary action, a struggle for liberation: liberation from partisan Spaniards, by annihilating the political parties; liberation of the Catalans and Basques, fighting against anything that prevents them from being and feeling fully Spanish; liberation of the workers, attracting them toward the national cause and annihilating injustice.

Catholic morality? That is not what this is about, comrades, for we are referring to a morality of preservation and magnification of "the Spanish," not merely "the human." We care more for saving Spain than saving the world. We care more about Spaniards than about mankind. All of this is because both the world and mankind are things we can approach as saviors only if we have achieved national fullness, if we have previously saved ourselves as Spaniards.

The fact that Spaniards—or many Spaniards—are Catholic does not mean that Catholic morality is the national morality.

Perhaps the traditional confusion around this explains a significant part of our ruination. It is not through Catholicism that we must approach Spain, but directly, without intermediaries of any kind. A Spanish Catholic is not necessarily a patriot simply because he is Catholic. He may also not be one, or his patriotism may be lukewarm.

The failure to account for this by the entire non-Catholic or indifferent Spain has perhaps deprived us, the Spaniards, of a national idea of direct elaboration. The dissenting elements— shall we call them the left?—have shown, in this and many other matters, that they were mere satellites of the other national sector—should we call it the right?—and that they have shaped their thinking by accepting the definitions provided by the latter.

Then, in effect, Catholics have always been identified with Spain, and they could not seriously imagine the existence of a Spanish national idea if not through the Church. In Spain, there has been a religious patriotism and a monarchical patriotism, but not a direct patriotism, not a popular patriotism arising from the masses and oriented toward them.

No, comrades, the national morality, the national idea as a duty, neither equates to religious morality, nor is it contrary to it. It is simply distinct, and it reaches all Spaniards simply because they are Spaniards, without having to be anything else.

### 5. Social Nationalism and National Socialism

The objective of winning the masses for a historical task of service to the Spanish fatherland is an achievable endeavor and must be actualized via the national revolution of the youth. The Spanish people are burdened with a thousand treacherous and lamentable propagandas, and how dearly they pay for paying mind to them and applauding them.

There they sit now, almost without a fatherland, and at the mercy of all the storms unleashed upon it by adventurers. However, the Spanish people have never truly heard a voice anguished by their misfortune, and for that reason, they have never rejected it. Confidence and faith in the people cannot be lost, as that would inexorably decree the final ruin of Spain, its incapacity to open the doors to a historical future.

Each era has its own mechanisms and peculiar efficiencies. Ignoring them means staying on the sidelines of success. Well, then, in this era, the masses are the unique instruments of national greatness. We can accept that in other times, now distant, powers unrelated to the heat of the masses managed to build powerful and prosperous fatherlands relying solely on their own genius. Spain is not the nation with the fewest examples of these achievements in its grand past.

The Spanish national revolution cannot do without the masses. It is false to think that our people will never accept a full and demanding national banner. Such thoughts come from those with small chests, whose voices are too weak and feminine to attract the strength of the masses. On the contrary, the Spanish masses are now waiting and calling for the presence of a true national voice.

What occurs is that a series of powerless and false voices are presented, tried, and tested, but their failure does not and cannot signify the failure of the national voice of Spain. The youth will easily gain the support of the masses if they can embody in their propaganda the current anguish of the people. They have been suffering the greatest calamities, and today, they are a poor people, exploited and martyred solely because they are exposed in history, without a national shelter, nor truly possessing a fatherland.

The nationalization of the masses in Spain is opposed, in essence, by two attitudes and forces that act by different means: one is constituted by groups that wish to disregard the masses and desire that Spain, the Spanish fatherland, should rely solely on them for support; the other is formed of all the groups, parties, and tendencies that seek to detach the Spanish people from any national concern, thus leaving them diminished and sadly playing the double role of defeated and deserter. Then, it always happens that extra-national masses fall under the whip of minorities with "suspect patriotism," or they are directly or otherwise enslaved by a foreign power.

The youth that orient their struggles toward the national revolution must not forget for a single minute that winning over the masses is an irreplaceable factor if they are to succeed, which is very distinct from seeking majority rule. It is not about this latter aspect, nor about the adherence of the masses to the national cause, since the cause of the Fatherland is a numerical problem. We will discuss this a little further ahead when we address the strategy that the youth should follow.

The nationalism of the masses, their acceptance of a national discipline, requires that the Fatherland genuinely become a liberating banner for them. The Spanish people suffer more than any other nation from the lack of strength in Spain. The current economy of our country is weak and almost resembles that of colonial economies. From that, profound evil arises, the effect of which is the extremely low standard of living of fifteen million Spaniards.

Spain possesses a rudimentary and treacherously rapacious capitalism that avoids all risks and lives completely outside any idea of serving the Spanish national economy. Our economy is not free, which is to say, it is hindered from adopting the forms and following the paths that would most benefit its own progress and the general well-being of the entire nation. The mining and agricultural industries tend to strengthen foreign economies, particularly that of England, more than they do our own. For half a century or more—in other words, during the period of imperialist economic expansion—Spain has not been free to direct its economy and has been obligated to serve the interests of other nations. The Spanish worker, the farmer, the industrialist, the entire population have labored under dismal conditions and suffered the consequences of Spain's lack of economic freedom.

A minority of Spaniards, hidden behind vast private estates, banks, and industrial enterprises directly supported by the state, have reaped enormous profits by exploiting the nation's weakness and enriching themselves at the expense of the anomalies and deficiencies upon which our entire economic organization is based. These individuals view the country's backwardness as magnificently lucrative.

There is hardly any industry, small or large. Our farmers, the vast majority of cultivators—especially since a strong demand for industrial goods from rural areas began fifteen or twenty years ago—have been shamelessly exploited, with their harvests usurped from them in exchange for overpriced manufactured goods; this has made it impossible for any productive capitalization to occur in the countryside.

We have two urgent needs before us, which can only be achieved through the national revolution: liberating the Spanish economy from the foreign oppression by organizing it solely for its own interest, and dismantling the current economic and financial system that operates to the benefit of those who have taken advantage of, and even embraced our weakness.

And, naturally, only a vigorous, energetic, and free Spain can seriously embark on the realization of such purposes. The foreign economic powers—principally the French and English—that currently control our entire production and external trade will always impose their will and voracity on a fragmented, divided, and weak Spain.

The youth cannot evade this question or engage in nationalist rhetoric without directly addressing the social-economic problem that currently renders us a nearly colonial and enslaved nation. Any other stance would be too grotesque, and it would prove to be impossible and entirely sterile. If one is committed to serving the national destiny of Spain, if one genuinely aspires to its greatness and truly desires to make Spain a free homeland, one of the primary battles must be to dismantle the existing economic order, which, we repeat, only favors audacious minorities with complete disregard for the genuine interests of the entire nation.

Spanish capitalism lacks sufficient strength to challenge the anomalies on which the national economy rests, and only undertakes ventures and enterprises for which it secures the support of the state beforehand. This shows nothing but incapacity, and it indicates that it is not possible to align the economic development of the Spanish people into its pace. How, then, can it even have the will to rectify this situation, if, as we mentioned, it benefits and takes advantage of Spain's stagnation and economic servitude?

In Spain, there is an unavoidable need to transfer the responsibility and historical task to the state, making it the one that, either by replacing private capital or by using it as a obligatory auxiliary at its service, increases industrialization in line with the nature of our economy. This would bring two formidable advantages: first, it would effectively achieve the economic progress that rightfully corresponds to Spain, taking into account the characteristics of its raw materials, international trade, and domestic market; secondly, it would carry out these advancements solely and exclusively for the benefit of all Spaniards, without financial oligarchies forcing or distorting these purposes according to their private interests.

This is true, and only in this way would Spain have a robust economy—which is to say, its railways would not be in ruins, it would have heavy industry, it would take advantage of its hydroelectric wealth, and it would avoid the shameful practice of exporting iron ore only to import it back as steel or expensive machinery. There would be no forced unemployment, it would have a maritime fleet like all other coastal nations, and as a European gateway to America, a continent that shares our language and has an agrarian economy, Spain would engage in substantial trade and economic relations therewith. We could have all of this, and that is not to mention Africa, another continent within our reach, which is asking to become one of the world's major objectives in the future.

To present such a panorama to a state and a regime like the one we have today in Spain is, in effect, absurd. Those who say that the state is a poor manager and an inefficient administrator are correct. However, we must add that these judgments apply fully to the democratic-bourgeois state, which is ineffective and absurd, but not to the institutions arising from the national revolution, nor to a legitimate political power emerging from the struggles carried out by the nation itself in a pursuit of liberation and greatness.

Such a political power as that can indeed achieve this with absolute efficiency and absolute integrity. It only needs to project itself onto the current sectors where the paralytic and inept zone of our economy manifests and resides: heavy industry, transportation, banking, and international commerce. If the national state were to directly control and nationalize these grand functions, the rapid prodigious growth of the Spanish economy, and consequently of private economies and the entire working class, would become an immediate reality.

It is not about spoliation or expropriation in the Marxist sense. Firstly, this is because the goal is not so much to seize existing wealth as it is to create new wealth, and secondly, because this would greatly invigorate the positions—which today find themselves exhausted and weak—of small industry, of domestic commerce, and of rural property, integrating them into an economic order of high consumption and mobility.

Without hesitation of any kind, comrades, the problem of the national revolution must be bound to the frank and bold adoption by the state of a guiding and preeminent role in the aforementioned economic tasks.

Spain stakes its independence and future on the possibility of carrying out boldly and without hesitation an economic plan based on those perspectives: if you will, based on state capitalism. Otherwise, it will continue to live off of a miracle, at the mercy of its enemies, with its population decimated, constituting a sad, failed possibility, a true historical disgrace.

## 6. Demographic Growth and Military Strength

We can only commence to seriously contemplate Spain's greatness when its population has at least doubled, and this greatness is indeed possible. Forty million Spaniards inhabiting our peninsula constitute an excellent guarantee of a prosperous economic and political future, even on a global scale. It is assumed that these forty million people would, of course, have access to food, clothing, and housing. In other words, they would have purpose in their fatherland; otherwise, it is a given that they would not have been born.

The demographic laws also have their inexorability. An exhausted population with no goal will hardly reproduce at a rapid pace. Spain has an extremely low population density—one hundred sixteen inhabitants per square mile—and despite that, even with less than half of the population it could sustain without overpopulation, one can say that the majority of Spaniards live in permanent scarcity. Furthermore, seven hundred thousand of them are unemployed.

The anomaly is so extraordinary that even stones would cry out. However, the historical juncture in which we find ourselves, as Spaniards, does not permit us to focus solely on devising a practical means for the well-being of the twenty-three million of us who currently exist.

Such an attitude is not at all paradoxical. It is closely tied to the aspirations for Spain to have a robust industry. The world experienced a rapid stage of population growth, and it was due to the beginning of the historical process of industrial mechanization.[18] Only an economically strong Spain can reach the required forty million inhabitants. This number of Spaniards would transform our peninsula into something it has not been until now, and it would prevent, among other things, our excellent maritime situation remaining almost useless. It would see to it that Spain turns into a major center of consumption, enabling it to become a trading nation as well. Currently, our ports and coasts have a very weak hinterland, which is the source of their paleness, poverty, and ultimately, the discontent of the national periphery.

Forty million Spaniards would live better than the current twenty-three million.

But there is more, and it is that the human factor is indispensable as an ingredient of the power and strength of the Fatherland.

Today, even the blind can see that it is a decisive matter, a matter of life or death for Spain, to increase its strength. The neighboring great powers exert, as we have said, an economic tyranny over our country. Furthermore, they will only respect this status quo that benefits them as long as they do not see or perceive a more effective way to exploit us. For on that day, they would tighten the screws even more on our people.

I am unfamiliar with any other effective means, comrades, to make Spain strong than to have a powerful army. The Spanish military policy, for many years, appears to have been designed with the clear intention of preventing Spain from having any military strength. Of course, a true army, an efficient military power, is impossible as a standalone endeavor. In the Spain of the last fifty years, lacking industry, lacking inhabitants, lacking unity, and lacking a national or international doctrine, an authentic, well-equipped, and sizable army would have been absurd.

---

[18] Consider some revealing figures: from the thirteenth to the eighteenth century—that is, for five hundred years—the population of Europe increased by 10 percent. However, during the last century, it has grown from 185 million to over 500 million; this increase represents almost 200 percent.

But in present-day Spain, in the light of the youth and the historical aspirations for national liberation, a robust militia, a grand army, is a primordial necessity. Now, this army and militia can only be conceived as a product of the population and as an armed projection of the nationalized popular spirit, not as an army of pure technique, detached from the rhythm and daily anguish of the Fatherland, a mute and lifeless witness.

The prevention and undermining of the spirit of the military, underestimating and destroying its essential characteristics, poses one of the greatest dangers to the strength of a nation. Anti-militaristic countries, those that fail to understand or appreciate the virtues of the military, are often the first to succumb to the tyranny of their own army. Such armies, having emerged and having been shaped in an atmosphere hostile to their own vitality, tend to possess inferior virtues in such cases.

Spain has suffered to a large extent from this anti-militaristic illness, this attitude of renouncing everything that involves collective heroism, interior discipline, and potential struggle. The new youth will have to dispel these seeds with their mere presence and overcome with vigor this true scourge of the recently prevailing opinion of the Spanish.

Indeed, Spain presents as one of the ingredients of its true genius a great physical and psychological capacity for the military. Throughout its finest days, Spain has been a nation of soldiers, exemplifying qualities of bravery and strategic acumen imperative for military life.

To deny Spaniards their inherent military destiny, to impede Spain from showcasing and providing its natural reservoir of soldiers to the military, is akin to severing one of its most robust branches. Throughout history, there have always been outbursts, unmistakable signs of resistance against this restriction. Even during the darkest days of the nineteenth century, Spaniards yearned to break free from these limitations. On numerous occasions, including the most monumental one—the War of Independence—they spontaneously, hero- ically, and simply unleashed their warrior spirit, as befits a nation with strong military traditions.

Moreover, our era, more abundantly than others, produces and gives rise to a type of people whose deepest desires and most intimate and outstanding qualities revolve around mili- tary dedication and the life of a soldier. Furthermore, social life today increasingly demands close-knit and rigid coexist- ence, disciplined cohesion, and uniformity. These facts de- nounce and reveal the trend toward a state of the spirit deep- ly inclined to understand the innermost essence of a soldier, a warrior.

But of course, by advocating for the revival of our military spirit, we do so, among other things, to free ourselves from deficient and mediocre militarism. The military, like poetry, is only valuable when it attains high qualities. Otherwise, it becomes completely detestable and insufferable.

Today, one of Spain's most urgent needs is to enter a pro- cess of militarization. This stems, in part, from its own inher- ent nature. It is also essential for historical efficacy, as it can only successfully undertake its national, economic, and politi- cal revolution by embracing certain militarized aspects. Above all, it is crucial for strengthening itself against external pres- sures, securing its freedom, and preserving its independence.

A Spain with forty million inhabitants, the only one that truly matters, would naturally boast heavy industry, a large merchant fleet, and robust agriculture, with abundant re- sources to equip an army capable of defending our rights against external enemies. It is crucial to remember that Spain would encounter enormous difficulties and formidable obsta- cles in its quest for economic and political power on the global stage, as it must overcome resistance from countries that cur- rently hold the world in their grip. Nevertheless, our military strength would remain solely defensive, dedicated to protect- ing Spain's right to be a free, wealthy, and prosperous nation. We would not need to initiate attacks or send our armies against others, but we must ensure that no external force mediates or keeps us in an eternal situation of defeat, oppressed by the greed of an inimical Europe.

## 7. The Pathways to International Strengthening

Our Spanish homeland is in a clear international situation. All judgments made about it can be accurate except one: that one that is confusing and difficult to explain.

The case of Spain is that of a country that, after a great defeat, has not been able to recalibrate and recover its international freedom. It is a country to which its enemies have guaranteed survival, but at the cost of its remaining fallen, poor, and weak.

It is well-known that Spain possesses, and has possessed at any point in time, sufficient spiritual and material energies to rebuild itself as a great world power. It would be erroneous to think that the reasons behind its failure to do so are internal, attributable to itself, thus falling into an absurd self-defeating mysticism or an inferiority complex. No, everything that has been accounted for in history gives way to a result of causes that can always be perfectly identified and denounced.

If Spain, after its first setback (1648), has remained on a downward trajectory without recalibrating as a great power, it is because someone has prevented it.[19]

It is not that I believe international politics should be exclusively guided and oriented by age-old secular resentments. No; like any policy, it must primarily obey current and contemporary reasons. However, all Spaniards should be aware of a grim historical truth, and that is that England, with the utmost coldness and with an icy demeanor, has systematically dismantled our empire and subsequently ensnared us in the

---

[19] In 1648, as a continuation of the Thirty Years' War, the Spanish were on the losing side of the Eighty Years' War, which was fought in the Habsburg Netherlands between Dutch rebels and Spain.

vise of national constriction, forcing us to remain stagnant and anchored. In this task, and with its proximity and caution as a heavily burdened power with many rivals, France has joined forces with England, and undoubtedly, these two nations have directly caused Spain's centuries-long secular postponement.

Spain has been fought against, surrounded, in the most cunning manner. Skillfully, its adversaries avoided making themselves overly visible, which is to say, they have avoided projecting to the Spanish people a sense of constant anxiety and danger. Except for the Napoleonic invasions—a mere mistake and blunder of the Bonapartist Empire—Spain has never felt an immediate, distressing, and real possibility of invasion. Thus, with the exception precisely of the War of Independence, a lesson not forgotten by Europe, Spain has been able to face the greatest external storms without flinching or being affected by them.

Spain has given its enemies a thousand ways to yoke us to their chariot: first, with its lack of bold direction in the internal lines of its policy; then, with the exacerbation of peripheral discontent, with the issue of regional autonomies; and above all, with its economic inertia, with the fact that we have resigned ourselves to entering the orbit of Franco-English conveniences, adopting the space assigned to us by these imperialisms.

However, Spain's international weakness and its dramatic resignation actually stemmed from its internal policies. The truth is that it has not resisted even in the slightest, nor has it hindered the development of external machinations, not even forcing them into more blatant intervention or actions. All the efforts of our neighbors—and England is our neighbor in three ways: Portugal, Gibraltar, and the ocean—were aimed at preventing Spain from ever achieving the status and importance of a great power.

Spain has not had, for the last century, a sufficiently robust political situation internally to break free from that grip.

The article in the 1931 Constitution stating that Spain renounces war is the culmination of servitude and amounts to a true offer to international piracy.[20]

What international paths would a successful national revolution follow today? It is conceivable that if an event were to occur in Spain with enough potency to break free from its centuries-old limitations and elevate the historical will of the Spanish people, it would immediately be hindered, sabotaged, by our neighbors.

The international possibilities that Spain has today are extremely limited. Among many other things that are denied to it—caused by, and don't forget, the prevailing political and social system—is the ability to have an international policy. Then, faced with bothersome situations, there are only two options: to accept them or to break them.

The problem is internal today, and it appears in a manner that may not have been seen before. Because for many years, Spain has not had a similar opportunity to genuinely attempt the definitive resolution of its terrible conflict.

If the internal victory were to occur, if Spain were to overcome its current internal crisis in favor of its national recovery, then the international prospects would become boundless. Spain would be daring in all respects and willing to take on any challenge: to reclaim Gibraltar, to unite the entire peninsula under one destiny, together with the great Portuguese nation (where the proponents of statutes, federations, and autonomous communities could indeed find a place), to draw a broad line of African expansion (the entire northern region of this continent, from the Atlantic to Tunisia, holds many Spanish dreams and much Spanish blood), to establish a political, economic, and cultural connection with the entire

---

[20] The Spanish Constitution of 1931 was the constitution of the Second Spanish Republic, which, among other things, made provisions for the democratic election of the heads of state and government. It was altogether progressive, democratic, and anti-clerical.

Hispanic block of our America, to become the possibility of a firm and just continental order for Europe itself.

It does not appear possible to achieve all of that while remaining in the arms of our traditional benefactors. Neither does it appear feasible if the current European powers conserve their strength. However, it doesn't appear illusory to think that things can change, as their preservation becomes increasingly challenging, and some of them are already on a historical path of decomposition.

Spain would have to wait, as mentioned before, to possess an international policy for some time, during which it can adopt only one policy: to avoid getting seriously entangled in the European maelstrom and not to join powers with a highly dubious fate in their catastrophe.

Today in Europe, there exists only one policy the future of which is unlikely to clash with ours. It is the policy of Germany, and it is highly convenient for Spain to keep an eye on its international moves, in case we discover a series of fertile interference.

But this could only happen with the utmost caution, because our Spain must avoid any commitment intersecting with its route toward ascension that would compromise or paralyze its progress.

# III

# STRATEGIC SCHEMES

What matters more than a clear idea of what is wanted is how it is to be achieved and by what infallible means can one arrive at its realization. A good path often leads to a splendid place, and it is already its own justification. The youth in Spain who are beginning to perceive the anguish of their destiny and are trying out gestures of action must give utmost attention to the problems related to their strategic route. For they are alone by an impulse, a driving force as the desire to give themselves and the country a historical push. However, they are not alone in other aspects, as in Spain there are other forces, ideas, entrenchments, interests, and so forth, among which it is necessary to move, overcoming some, neutralizing others, and assimilating the rest.

## 1. Political Action

The Spanish youth, as historical subjects of the national revolution, must above all choose, without the possibility of another option, as the field and theater of their presence, this: political action. And this, not to align themselves with the current parties or to serve in the slightest the issues they raise, but with a dual purpose: first, to overpower and take control of the governing areas, where the powers most directly responsible for Spain's inertia entrench themselves, and second, to camp within the very center of popular effectiveness, in the real whirlwind of the masses.

It isn't in science, religion, professional expertise, domestic worship, or sports where action and presence of the youth should manifest itself in the anomalous situation of the nation: *it is in political action.* Here, their energies must converge, considering those other pursuits as valuable but subordinate to the objectives of the national revolution, which are primarily political in nature. They must recognize that those pursuits are inoperable, partial, and inadequate for the historical tasks that correspond to our situation today.

Spain will not regain its great destiny, nor will the Spaniards regain their dignified life, *with swiftness and urgency*, through the path of wisdom, nor through religious mission, nor through professional preparation, nor by the mere fact that everyone become a good athlete. *Even if all of that were achieved*, it could very well coexist with Spain's historical disgrace, with its servitude, its degradation, and its international slavery.

The helm of swiftness, of urgency, is what permits the dismantling, the overcoming of the dominant political power, replacing it, and undertaking with the Spanish masses the historical edification and conquest of the Fatherland. That requires engaging in political action, even with the evident purpose of reducing to ashes deceitful and disastrous partisan politics.

To present to the youth the path of political action is to demonstrate to them the place where the historical helm they precisely need resides. It is where the electric transformer lies—a transformer that, in inept, insensitive, or treacherous hands, causes dramatic blackouts, but in capable and devoted hands, ignites and illuminates historical routes.

There is no worse skepticism, nor a more pernicious and impotent doctrine for the youth, than falling into isolation, disillusionment, and inactive contempt for political engagements and effectiveness. Those who adopt such an attitude condemn themselves irreversibly to a permanent limbo, an eternal infancy of imbeciles and castrated souls.

The primary strategic concern, therefore, is the creation of a well-armored organ of political action, resistant to the allure of temptations, disdainful of conspiracies, and capable of delivering a definitive blow to the political machinations of the parties upon which the current state is founded and supported. Engaging in politics is not about merely being rivals of one party or another, but maintaining a permanent and absolute rivalry with the entire system. It is politics *against* politics, party *against* parties.

## 2. Direct Action

That the youth must adopt a tactic of direct action, meaning an ethic of distrust towards anything that does not originate from them and a determination to impose new norms by themselves, is indeed unquestionable. This is implicit in the attitude we mentioned earlier, which corresponds to our youth: the attitude of a soldier. Soldiers always practice direct action, and by their very nature, they are the only ones who truly embody its great fecundity and significance.

The youth, as a sector of society, are also the only ones who impart to direct action not a particularistic sense of exacerbation and excess of one class, but rather a character that is wholly national and human, the profound justification of their violence toward parasitic values and toward intermediaries equipped with degradation.

Direct action will guarantee to our youth liberation from all parliamentary myths, from all reverence toward what doesn't deserve respect, and from all submission before empty and false idols. They will always be in danger, exposed, living a full ascetic life of great emotional grandeur, and experiencing great historical empowerment.

In the practice of direct action, something of utmost urgency in our fatherland is also accomplished: the possible mergence and selection of new ruling minorities, arising from and representing the masses, who replace, by their own authentic right of conquest, the traditional minorities or those originating from dominant political parties and sects.

Direct action is not always, nor is it equivalent to, armed violence. It is primarily the support for an attitude of rupture, an ethic of rigid justice against decrepitude or treason, and a complete, total trust in what is incorporated and brought forth.

Violence, rupture, will have a profound echo of moral achievement, heroism, firmness, and integrity in our youths, as they are the ones who will bring forth and drive the national revolution.

Precisely for this reason, three justifications, three dimensions can be attributed to the violence of the youth, and any one of them would be enough to self-justify in a sufficient manner:

a) As a moral value of rupture, as detachment and rebellion against decrepit, treasonous, and unjust values.

b) As a necessity, which is to say, as an obligatory principle of defense, as an unavoidable tactic in the presence of enemy encampments (Spain today is filled with true encampments, ready for war).

c) As proof, as a demonstration of integrity, capability, and the historical legitimacy that moves the soldiers of the national revolution.

These justifications prevent the direct action of the youth from falling into crime, banditry, and culpable political action, which is always associated with an individual, anarchic sign, and small visionary groups.

But let us draw some interesting consequences from the third of these justifications:

### 3. The Ruling Minority, the Political Power Spain Needs

One of the historical teachings that can be obtained from the democratic-bourgeois world cycle is the demonstration that the social type from which a great nation derives its ruling minority, its governing political body, is not trivial.

Not everyone, not all social groups offer guarantees of understanding and serving the general and historical interests of the nation in a profound manner, and when we talk about the nation, we can also refer to the entire populace. Liberal and parliamentary democracy entrusts the governing mission to the representative elements of its own system, which are skeptical and engage in a tug-of-war—in other words, to lawyers.

The struggles for the national revolution, and the strategy pursued in them, must take these facts into account to ensure that their triumph does not result in the deception of leaving the revolution without its own management, without faithful leaders.

Spain is one of the nations that must entrust its destiny to those who interpret its own essence with the utmost rigor and fidelity. Only then will it effectively render fruitful consequences of a historical order. The national revolution, therefore, must not forget that it itself must produce and create its own governing minority, to whom the great nationalized masses can entrust the task of manifesting transformations and guiding the ship of the national state with resilience and good spirits.

Now more than ever, and especially in Spain, both due to its historical expression and its unique future, it is necessary for the state to be in the hands of men with characteristics entirely different from those typically possessed by democratic-bourgeois politicians.

This proof, therefore, this demonstration that we ascribed to the direct action of the national-revolutionary youth, is related to this reality, to this need to highlight and put at the forefront of the state men of proven integrity, proven fidelity, and profound anguish and concern for the historical destiny through successful action and management as creators and leaders of the direct action of the national forces in struggle.

These characteristics, which in a certain sense correspond to the man of the military, are not, however, those of the soldiers in normal armies under bourgeois-parliamentary regimes—elements that are generally bureaucratized, pacifistic, narrow-minded, and without sharpness or historical vision. Instead, these characteristics are produced by the masses and extracted from within the people, as the flawed course of the time in which they emerge prevents them from being incorporated into official life; in other words, they remain in opposition.

In Spain, we are facing this phenomenon. We live in an oppressive monopolization of public life by lawyers, bureaucrats, defeatists, and those mentally disabled by profession.

That is why the youth must recognize the need to make way for human values of more appropriate coloration for the governing task. They must step out of their struggles and stand out in them. If these struggles consist of peaceful exhortations to domestic life and faithful fulfillment of civic duties, it is better to not move, to continue in progressive paralysis, and let the lawyers, bureaucrats, and good bourgeoisie perform their honorable function as the definitive liquidators of the Fatherland.

The tasks that can be assigned to Spain's immediate future require that a team of seasoned and hardened Spaniards stand at its forefront: individuals forged and tempered in days of integrity. We need men with not the slightest capacity for trembling, fraud, and historical myopia.

## 4. The Issue Does Not Lie with Majorities

The mystique of the masses is not the mystique of majorities. The Spanish national revolution cannot be executed or achieved by relying solely on the mobilization of majorities. The commitment to convince the majority of Spaniards beforehand may be legitimately required to change a right-wing policy to a left-wing one or for some frivolity, but it is inadequate and infantile to expect it from the executors of the national revolution.

And this is due to many reasons, both because it is not the obligation of numerical majorities to be direct depositaries or guardians of the national historical destiny, and because majorities are not necessary for triumph. The concept of majority is, indeed, merely a tool for political victory, suitable for liberal democratic systems. But it is nothing more than that. Beyond the scope of liberal democracy, the term "majorities" as a political term or concept lacks any meaning whatsoever.

Therefore, the national revolution stands apart from such a question. The strategic line should not revolve around the conquest of majorities, but rather around a different set of values. On one hand, it involves the mobilization of the masses with greater national density and significance, and on the other hand, the revolutionary mechanisms that pave the way to power.

The masses, yes. They constitute an indispensable collaboration. The masses can rally around a flag and a slogan, even achieve victory, and yet still be a minority. Such differentiation must be made clear from the perspective of the national revolution. It must prevail not by being a numerical majority, but by the perfectionism, mobilization, effort, and combativeness of its masses.

The Spaniards who actively and tirelessly strive for the national greatness of Spain, who wish to free their compatriots from international slavery, who desire a resurgence of the moral, economic, and cultural life of their homeland, and so forth, may perhaps be a minority for a long time—and not because there is a hostile majority against them, with an antinational consciousness and a will for self-annihilation. No. Rather, it is logical that there are broad inert zones, insensitive to the meaning of those problems: inert, but not inimical. Well, let us not forget that the issues affecting the national revolution are distinct from purely individual and private matters. Therefore, they may escape the understanding of the great majorities, except in exceptional moments when the national historical will converges fully with the near and concrete aspirations of the entire people. This is the best climate for the national revolution, and fortunately, it is the one that is now securely emerging in our Spanish homeland.

### 5. The Reality of the Spanish People

That powerful forces oppose the national revolution is an evident fact. It is also clear that it would have to adopt a tough and bitter profile with certain sectors of Spanish social life. However, the national revolution would be the least bloody and least rancorous among those that are currently looming and threatening to unchain themselves. We know to what extent it is unjust to make our contemporaries culpable, both for the historical misfortune of Spain, and for the economic misery and backwardness in which we find ourselves.

Therefore, it seems to us an enormous injustice to claim that the vindictive blade should fall directly upon any group or class. The Marxist attempt to ravage the Fatherland with strong violence against supposed culprits deserving extermination appears both erroneous and criminal. Such a notion is senseless, and it will not correspond to the fact that a small part of the strategic motivations of the national revolution may aim to prevent and halt the actualization of Marxism in revolutionary rivalry with its purposes. We firmly believe that the Spanish people, the Spanish society, does not present any sector today to which we can exclusively assign all the responsibility. There is neither an entirely exploitative bourgeoisie nor entirely deracinated labor movement here. Those who approach the reality of our fatherland with morbid images from other countries and attempt to apply equally morbid formulas and tactics are undoubtedly of no service to the Spanish national revolution. On the contrary, we must delve into the intimate and profound anguish of the Spanish people, the entire people, and perceive the different groups and classes, each with their own historical context, needing liberation and assistance.

This position of the national revolution, which excludes any a priori and comprehensive struggle against classes and generic values, and projects all its violence against those who stand outside its relentless service to the destiny of the Fatherland, wherever the transgressors are and whoever they may be, is the true position of love for the Spanish people as a whole, the authentic liberating banner that enhances the spirit of our nation.

### 6. The Catholic Church and Its Interference with the National Revolution

Before, we mentioned the need to address the issue of Catholicism and its interference with the political and revolutionary endeavors of the national youth. This topic may be difficult and delicate, but we must confront it and derive strategic consequences from it.

The Church can be considered a witness to the birth of Spain as a historical entity. It is connected to the culminating moments of our national past and, in many respects, linked in a profound manner to high-quality Spanish institutions. Additionally, it is an institution that possesses some positive political advantages, such as its capacity for collaboration and service, given that it finds and engages with sufficiently astute authorities capable of appreciating its contributions and possessing the strength to accept them without risk.

It appears unquestionable that Catholicism is the religion of the Spanish people, and they have no other. To undermine it, its strict spiritual and religious significance, would be equivalent to attacking something fundamental to the people, and such an affront can never be justified by those who embrace the national perspective. All of this is crystal clear and difficult to refute, even for those who are not bound by any religious discipline or hold any particular sympathy for the Church.

With that ends the so-called declaration of principles of the national revolution concerning the Catholic religion. Attempting to go beyond these principles in one way or another would disfigure the spirit of the national victory and even put it at risk, jeopardizing its achievement.

The task of building a national doctrine, a plan for historical resurgence, a strategy of struggle, and effective political institutions can exist without solely appealing to the Catholic identity of Spaniards. Not only that, but Catholics can and should collaborate in this endeavor, and serve it, in the name of their national grandeur, in the name of their patriotism, and not for any other reason.

Furthermore, don't forget that the national revolution aims to discover a bundle of Spanish truths, both of a national and social nature, which can and must be embraced by the entire nation, without the possibility of criticism or dissent. We know that the historical life of Spain depends on the validity of this bundle of grand and indisputable principles, which ensures its moral unity and cohesion. Precisely, the national revolution finds its justification in the current absence of these consensuses within the spirit of our people.

Before, the moral unity of Spain was almost synonymous with the Catholic unity of the Spaniards. Whoever seriously pretends that today we can still aspire to such equivalence demonstrates how clouded their own personal desires are. No;

now it occurs that only under the banner of bourgeois and parliamentary democracy, that is, only under the influence of a liberal democratic political system, could Spain live or barely survive without a profound national solidarity, without moral unity.

The task of creating it, propagating it, and urgently establishing its principles is one of the highest historical purposes of this moment when we are, without doubt, witnessing the ruin and irremediable decrepitude of that system, and the impossibility of Spanish life under the governance of those without faith, spectators, and the incredulous.

We ask for faith and a national creed: social efficacy for the entire nation. We know that only through this approach can we wield victorious instruments and avoid descending into vile tyranny while establishing national obligation and loyalty to Spain's historical destinies for everyone. In the name of the Fatherland and the social liberation of all the people, we would not hesitate in making any decision, no matter how grave and bloody. However, the Church would tremble today—and rightfully so—at the thought of any coercive action against the unbelievers.

The national revolution is an undertaking to be accomplished as Spaniards, and the Catholic life is a matter to be fulfilled as men, to save the soul. Therefore, let no one twist or confuse these matters, as they are extremely distinct. It would be agonizingly regrettable if the banners were twisted, and this juncture in Spain's history were resolved in futile struggles reminiscent of the nineteenth century.

Spain, comrades, needs patriots who do not attach labels. There are many suspicions—and more than suspicions—that patriotism in the embrace of churches gets adulterated, debilitated, and corroded. The yoke and the arrows, emblematic of struggle, advantageously replace the cross to preside over the days of the national revolution.

### 7. *The Contribution of the Workers,*
### *the Spanish Working Class*

It is evident that one of the main goals of the national revolution is and must be the nationalization of the workers, meaning their incorporation into the historical enterprise that Spain represents. The broader and more vigorous the foundation of the national state, the greater the firmness and the efficacy in pursuing its historical purpose.

If the anguished and sensitive youth, concerned about Spain's misfortunes, decide to take energetic action to fortify and liberate the country, they must seek support and collaboration, more persistently than others, from the workers, the wage earners, the small farmers, and finally all those common Spaniards engaged in a constant and difficult struggle with life.

Precisely, the national revolution is the only banner under which the various people of Spain can come together, considering it as their own. They seek solutions not only for their particular problems, but also for that greater problem of Spain, which encompasses all the others.

The incorporation of the workers into Spain's national cause would offer enormous historical prospects. Not only can we not do without them, but it is also necessary to extract revolutionary fighters and patriots from the working class at all costs. It would be truly lamentable if the national revolution failed to achieve their support, as it would almost entirely invalidate its purpose.

All the endeavors that are necessary in Spain today, if it is to find its historical elevation and national victory, coincide almost entirely with the interests of the hardworking Spanish masses. No other can raise the flag of historical liberation as high as they can, and no one else needs, with greater urgency, to unite their destinies with that of the Fatherland. In the struggles against foreign economic imperialism, and against the parasitism of large rentiers, the position that benefits the workers aligns perfectly with the national interest.

The strategy of the national revolution concerning workers' organizations presents enormous difficulties that can only be overcome with honesty, decisiveness, and a profound sense of true Spanish interests. Due to various reasons—a less robust middle class, a deficient patriotic atmosphere in the country, and significant confusion surrounding the national cause— Spain requires the exceptional cooperation of the workers. The national youth will find themselves obligated, more than in other nations, to impart a strong social character to their revolution, embracing all the progress needed for the incorporation of the working class. Ah! But they must also be unwavering and stern with the deceitfully misled groups, who strive to shed their blood for utopian proletarian fantasies and the web of Moscow-inspired espionage that obstructs the Spanish masses' conscience and clouds their national fidelity.

I do not suppose that it is not altogether impossible for the youth to find large contingents of workers to the national cause they represent. Workers will perceive the youth's cause more swiftly and enthusiastically than others. They are more open to accepting new flags without being burdened by the excessive pressures of inherited ideas and family ties, as is the case with most other classes, whose notion of Spain is already bound to traditional and dead paths.

# IV

# FINAL CALL TO THE YOUTH

The forward march of the youth is a global agenda. They are thus becoming the historical agents of victorious upheavals everywhere. Thanks to them and their intervention, Europe has ousted Marxism and unveiled a new revolutionary approach, built on national strength, the dignity of the masses, and the construction of a new order.

At this moment, Spain offers a problem, without the possibility of postponement for rectification. After April 14th, which in itself lacked any transmutative significance, those aspiring to carry out and lead the immense transformations that will soon take place in Spain are already showing their profiles. By October 6th, a proletarian determination to participate in the upcoming Spanish juncture had already been displayed. Hence, the national presence is urgently needed, the national response that the youth must provide for that date.

The situation of the Fatherland is conclusive: The historic moment is rapidly approaching when it will be time to decide under which banner the transformations will take place. There are those who already wield the mallet with zeal. So we, raising our voice as loudly as possible and surrounding it with maximum emotion, say to the current youth of the Fatherland:

The approaching historical rectification must be carried out, executed, and nurtured by all of you, contesting step by step with other contenders for the purpose of the national revolution.

This solemn moment of Spain, in which its destiny will be vented out, perhaps for more than a hundred years, coincides with the period and moment of your lives when you are young, vigorous, and fearsome.

Could it be that the Fatherland and the people are left defenseless, as the liberators, patriots, and revolutionaries do not occupy their post?

Could it be that in forty or fifty years, those Spaniards who are young today and will be elderly then will look from a distance with anguish and sadness, realizing how the significant opportunity of this moment was squandered, how it ended in failure, all because of their cowardice, their desertion, their weakness?

## First Digression on the Revolutionary Sign of the Youths

### 1. The Presence of the Youth

In classical Greece, there was a historian who only spoke in his books about contemporary events. He sincerely believed, with magnificent naivety, that in the past, in earlier times, nothing of historical significance worth mentioning had occurred in the world. History, then, began in his own era, and its first pages had to correspond to the most notable events that unfolded before his eyes: in this case, the Peloponnesian Wars.[21]

Well then, this book, which is naturally consistent with the purpose of interpreting the profound reality of Spain and its immediate future under the historical banner of the national youth, must examine a phenomenon similar to that classical example. This will serve us in identifying the true presence of this new motivating force of history, which is the youth.

A youth-driven consciousness is at work when it holds a somewhat messianic view of itself—in other words, when it genuinely believes that its vigorous presence in history coincides with the final hours of an agonizing process of decomposition and crisis; when, in short, like the Greek, it perceives nothing before it but chaos and darkness. At that point, the consciousness of the youth realizes that its mere presence, its appearance, signifies a possibility for salvation and greatness: a dawn for the new world.

Repeatedly, perhaps most of the time, that belief, that assessment and estimation of their own destiny held by the youth, is an illusory display, resolved in pure fantasy, without a concrete mission to which it can ascribe. There are periods and moments when the presence of the youth as such is scarcely perceptible. Men barely pause in their youth and rapidly progress from infantile adolescence to maturity. Yet, entering into maturity, socially conforming to it, implies finding the existing forms acceptable and collaborating in their historical destiny, in the task of ensuring a broader permanence.

## 2. Conservative Eras and Revolutionary Eras

Thus, we are dealing with conservative and tranquil eras. The youth barely exist, as they are easily and swiftly reab-

---

[21] Thucydides is the historian that the author references here. He is widely considered the first historian whose works were based on a scientific method of writing history, based on his impartiality, material linking of cause and effect, use of historical evidence, and the avoidance of assigning causation to divine origins.

sorbed without difficulty into the normal tasks that preoccupy the world when they emerge. These are the culminating moments of empires, even as they have the slow declines that follow them in sight. Such was the case in Augustan Rome. Such was the case in the mid-sixteenth century Spain and the lengthy, anguishing process of subsequent decomposition. Such is the present time in England. Such was almost the entirety of the global nineteenth century.

The spirit and mission of the youth are thus camouflaged, or better yet, declared disruptive, strident, and demonic. Perhaps it appears in individual rebellions and is settled in literary romanticism, or if it adopts a political form, it becomes empty anarchism.

However, it can occur that this messianic consciousness of the youth, to which we have referred, strengthens and overflows in an overwhelming manner when, indeed, their presence truly coincides with a historical juncture of such decomposition that the vigorous emergence equates to an overwhelmingly fertile driving force.

This occurs and happens in eras of transformation, in revolutionary times, those in which the world manages to strangle the hydra of a process of decomposition or anguish and make way for a new order. These are eras of invention and conquest: creative periods that draw back the curtain and unveil new paths that history offers to the people.

Well, then, the historical subject of such moments, the impelling and accomplishing arm of theirs, is what we call the active consciousness of the youth. And to the extent that they influence and support with their distinct attributes—namely, the spirit of sacrifice, purity, fervor, and effort—the institutions and forms of the new system, the historical juncture accomplishes and fulfills its mission, either resolving into goals of fulfillment, or regressing and distorting its purpose.

The fact that the world—and above all the European nations, which are truly its most faithful expression—finds itself today under the sign of such a juncture, where the youth appear with a full messianic consciousness, self-suggested and self-elevated, causes this phenomenon to pass through a zone of clarity and become understandable to us. I find myself in the current, and it is within it that the fact presents itself to me in its entirety.

### 3. The Messianic Consciousness of the Youth

To convert the youth into the primary subject of history, the era necessarily adopts revolutionary profiles. Major revolutions have taken place in such moments, whether they are of a religious nature or of an economic and political character.

Naturally, the fact of the youth, the concept of the young, is elastic and flexible, above all when we refer to it in the manner that we do. Earlier, we alluded to eras that are in essence conservative and tranquil, during which the youthful stage of a person's life is transient, a brief flash in ones existence. On the contrary, in times of significant transformations, and when the grand revolutionary principles are projected onto nations, the first social fact that emerges is that the "process of duration" of youth elongates and expands considerably.

Then it can be said that man is "young" for a longer period of time, meaning he experiences appetite, emotions, restlessness, and anguish of youth over an extended timeframe. As youths transition into the decisive driving force, evolving into a creative subject, their mission, which in other eras may seem almost nonexistent as such, expands and dilates in an extraordinary manner, as it becomes, in fact, the very mission of humanity in that hour. A role like this, a task like this, cannot be trusted to fleeting social forces, but rather to men who will endure for longer. Hence, in terms of their mentality, customs, way of life, and concerns, during times and moments like those we refer to, man regards himself as, and indeed is, "young" until the age of fifty and beyond.

In those ages, he doesn't fully embed himself into the existing order; he still considers himself enlisted among those who seek and strive for the discovery of political, economic, or religious forms equipped with the effectiveness he yearns for. Indeed, he is discontented, displaced, dissatisfied. Naturally, in his historically most fertile stage, he is a soldier of the revolution that occurs during these times, always emerging victoriously.

Those are the people who constitute the core of the great revolutions and who, in one way or another, bear the responsibility of nourishing their military predominance, the historical mission of driving the monumental shifts and changes that occur in the world. They are the revolutionary phalanx of Julius Caesar, who conquer the rotted oligarchies of the Roman Republic and establish the Empire in the name of the masses. They are the illiterate and hungry Spanish conquerors of the sixteenth century, and those who enlist in the famous *tercios* that, under Charles V, affirm Spanish might in Europe. They are the Napoleonic troops that impose the tenets of the French Revolution across Europe. And finally, they are the decisive players today, not just in terms of execution and service, but in totality, drawing solely from themselves, generating leaders, norms, institutions, and their own historical goals.

## 4. Facing Subversive Juncture

Indeed, the world is currently undergoing a phase that precisely aligns with the characteristics described here. In today's context, the profiles that signal the active presence of a youth consciousness, infused with an unwavering messianic belief in its own destiny, have become more distinct across nearly the entire global landscape. As a result, we find ourselves immersed in an intense revolutionary atmosphere, marked by such fervor and strength that, to the surprise of many, certain inclinations from even the staunchest conservatism are now contributing to this revolutionary and subversive sentiment.

A brief analysis of the events today unmistakably confirms the accuracy of our judgments. The presence of the youth indeed saturates the global landscape. Their issues permeate every corner, and the dilatory trait of the duration of "youthfulness" is evident, as we previously showed: a distinctive feature of historical junctures characterized by revolutionary and subversive undertones.

For over fifteen years, let us say since the end of the Great War, there has been a mobilization of youth. As they gained momentum and prominence, they have coalesced and polarized into endeavors of varying natures according to circumstances. Yet they consistently leave a trail of transformations, some more successful than others, which have imparted and continue to impart a profoundly revolutionary sensation to the world.

### 5. The Lack of Solidarity Among Youth

Indeed, as the youth's numerical proportion expands, encompassing a larger span of human life, they are increasingly perceived as displaced and distant from any possibility of service and dependence on the prevailing order and system. This is due to two reasons: frequently, it occurs that there is no place for the youth, they are not readily accepted, and their initial impression often involves the stress of finding themselves without just appeals, almost in a role of historical residue. Additionally, there is another reason: the youth are often marked by an innate aversion to the social voids reserved for them. After a period of perplexity and critical orientation, they sometimes assume the tasks assigned to them; at other times, in open rebellion and adventure, they align and enroll themselves with the most compelling form of subversion they encounter.

Such a phenomenon, such a process, holds today the rank and character of a global event. It unfolds and reaches its climax in some nations, while timidly surfacing in others, but undoubtedly forming the most decisive driving force of the era.

In such a situation, the youth confront the fundamental reality of their existence; they enter the battlefield, then, for their dilemma can scarcely be resolved in any other way than with the firm determination to forge their own path. They realize they have entered a repellent world, defective and submerged in hundreds of miseries. However, they do not belong to it; they stand outside its walls, bearing an irrevocable and invaluable baggage: their vitality, their fervor, and above all, their immunity to any depression or pessimistic solution. As it so happens, in such a juncture, the youth find themselves caught between a rock and a hard place: they reject the prevailing order and system, but simultaneously, they are shut off from all pessimistic exits, all forms of resignation. This is their moment in history, and it prohibits them from retreating in the face of their own destiny.

Therefore, the youth who manage to embrace a complete messianic awareness, after experiencing dissatisfaction and anguish with the prevailing forms, fully adopt a revolutionary stance, dedicated to serving the social, political, or religious transmutations that are destined to arise in such times.

Revolutionary eras—and the current one is more so than any—begin to reveal themselves through the symptoms that we are precisely highlighting here. The youth confront the panorama presented to them, following the norms of the purest classical profile. They believe in themselves, in the positive and fertile aspects of their presence, while devaluing and underestimating what came before them, what they bury in the darkness. This is how the revolutionary process reaches its culmination. The detachment of the youth from the established universal order becomes evident across all domains.

The significance of all this is clear: the preeminent values of a cultural, economic, and political nature appear before the youth devoid of brightness. They are false values, unworthy of any respect, and in their eyes, these values play the role of mere appearances of virtue serving degraded realities. In fact, they revolt against the kind of stagnant and mediocre life that is offered to them. Naturally, they reject the tasks seemingly assigned to them by the old groups, who still govern the existing forms.

### 6. Neither Moral Crisis, Nor Corruption, Nor Adventurism

And it is worth noting a phenomenon that accompanies this hostile attitude of the youth: they appear frequently under a morally depressive sign, surrounded by attributes suggestive of corruption and impurity. This is what is then termed, from the anti-youth and anti-historical perspective, the "moral crisis of youth." Perhaps the youth indeed tend toward a way of life that, for others, for representatives of static forms, is pure adventurous cynicism, pure corruption, pure escapism from the duty and difficulty of being industrious, disciplined, and obedient.

But that is merely another symptom of the historical shift, of the rupture that will be brought about by revolutions. This supposed corruption is simply ignorance and blindness to certain inhibitory norms. It bears no resemblance, then, to genuine corruption and dishonesty, characteristic of those who transgress moral norms that are not only not alien to them, but are created and forged by them, or at the very least, presented by them as the fundamental pillars on which their worldview and life rest.

Therefore, this accusation leveled against the active youth, presenting their resistance to embedding themselves in orthodox systems upon arrival as stemming from impure origins, is false and unjust. Their nonchalance, their affiliation with unconstrained norms, their breach of certain rituals, even the apparent ease with which they engage with old corrupting powers—none of this equates to the absolute moral degradation which it is usually labeled as.

We reject as invalid and mistaken the inclination to judge the "uprooting" of these youth as a sign of moral depression. Instead, it may be that they lack what can be called the bundle of current virtues. However, along with this "uprooting" that we mentioned, it doesn't exclude seeing them pursue new virtues and also being deeply connected to disciplines of significant grandiosity. Take heed that the revolutionary rupture they live in detaches them from one dogma before a new and different one has been created. The driving forces acting in such times experience an interregnum between the moment of their deviation from static forms and their adherence to a new moral discipline. With this, and considering what I previously explained about the characteristics of true corruption, it should become perfectly clear how the youth cannot be labeled as lax or degraded for carrying out their transformative function with styles that might outwardly appear adventurous. There are evident differences between a thief or highway robber and a revolutionary leader who, according to their social myth, seizes private fortunes in certain cases.

Their messianic, salvational character, and the sense that their presence in history occurs at the precise moment to prevent an irreparable catastrophe, constitutes the emotional basis of the youth. The chaos among them, the swamp, and the injustices they witness so clearly lead to their initial determination to assume the messianic role of saviors, of inaugurators of history, in the style of the Greek historian.

## 7. The Rupture of "Progress"

Thus, revolutionary eras are not truly progressive periods. There is neither a myth nor an illusion of progress where there is no continuous aspiration, no service to pre-existing values. It is not a matter of progress, as it is not today, but of tearing apart the veil of inventions. The journey is toward conquering situations and ways of life beneath which the ground is never firm, nor is there a permanent or even temporary stay in intermediate places.

On the contrary, it is the broad historical processes with a conservative character that are realized and accomplished under a function of progress, with a progressive mission. Progress is the son and product of collaboration, of continuity, precisely the two things that disappear and are denied under the dominion of triumphant youth. These youth break their solidarity with the most immediate past, which is to say, they refuse to carry on tasks already initiated—they refuse to steer the symbolic ship of progress.

Certainly, it should be evident how this digression effectively reveals the characteristics of the current era, the one we are experiencing right now, and in which we all act, in one way or another. Undoubtedly, one of the most noteworthy phenomena today is the remarkable extension of the youthful phase of men, accompanied by a range of moral, economic, and political implications. These expanded and intensified youth are progressively aligning themselves with their mission and are authentic representatives of this historical moment. They exert influence everywhere, harnessing the most spirited, heroic, and fertile qualities, and thereby indicating the direction they must take with great urgency. This trajectory is, beyond doubt, a revolutionary path, remarkably transformative and subversive. There's hardly a nation untouched by their emergence, and only a handful of strongholds resist their influence. It is important to clarify that we're not merely discussing temporary youthful mobilizations; rather, it goes beyond that, transcending into a more profound historical endeavor than a narrow interpretation of "youthfulness" would imply. Revolutionary periods introduce a mystique of youth that connects with the most pivotal part of their mission: facilitating the emergence of a world infused with youthfulness, which is to say, characterized by vitality and purity.

### Second Digression on the Current Profile of Europe

Today, Europe is, almost totally, the base of operations for the youthful and revolutionary spirit we referred to in the first digression. It won't be difficult for us to individually highlight, one by one, the culminating events in contemporary Europe, to point out the myths that orient and inspire, to examine the demeanor and concerns, while also demonstrating how all these elements—events, myths, actions, and concerns—are genuine products and direct manifestations of subversive youth.

For the past fifteen years, Europe has lived, in one way or another, devoted to the transmutative experience. Self-messianic youth are imposing their characteristics day by day, and winning battles against the old powers.

I am one of those who believe that Europe has barely entered the final stage of revolutionary achievements, and that that is why the episodes that already appear to be a product and a harvest in some definitive way—that is, calming and restricting episodes of historical subversion, already obtained from it itself—are rather flowerings and representative attempts of the new order and of the new system yet to come. If we review everything that has occurred in Europe, whether formally or episodically, we will notice that it is imbued with the same essence, responding to a style of rebellion, of rupture, and constantly dreaming of interpreting radical novelties. This is evident both in ideological directions and in manifestations of a more superficial and external nature. In addition, it is only by deploying the typical and even brutal mechanisms of transformative eras, along with their baggage of heroism, imposition, and determination, that the terrifying obstacles of this age have perhaps been tackled and even overcome.

What do we truly see in Europe? After the Great War, which served as the wake-up call that opened and inaugurated the subversive process, the following significant events have emerged in Europe. A precise understanding of these events is indispensable for those who wish to have a clear idea about the current European situation: post-war pacifism; Russian Bolshevism; Italian Fascism; German socialist racism; Marxist revolutionary impotence; decomposition of bourgeois economic and political institutions; forced unemployment; political homogenization of the masses.

Quickly and swiftly, we will evaluate these phenomena, unravel their meaning, and fit them into the ongoing global process under the influence of the large masses of youth.

### 1. Pacifism, the League of Nations, and French Imperialism

#### The Two Pacifisms

In the Great War, around ten million men were sacrificed. Truly, if someone could demonstrate that all those lives were sacrificed capriciously, without a profound and true connection to the most authentic and solemn intentions of history, we would have to declare without a moment's delay the stupidity and brutality of the Europe that declared and waged the war. Then, as if that demonstration had been made, an attitude of pacifism surfaced, grew, and developed throughout Europe, whose spectacle, when viewed from a distance, appears as the most repugnant requiem that could be dedicated to the millions of men who died in battle.

Never before in the entire course of history has there occurred, after a war, an environment of such moral wretched-
ness and such crisis of integrity as the one brought about by
the pacifist atmosphere following 1918. We can distinguish
two pacifisms: one, the diplomatic pacifism of the states; the
other, the naïve pacifism that sought to embed itself among
the broad popular masses. The first found its home and locus
in Geneva under the name of the League of Nations. The second attempted to instill in people's minds the belief that the
last war must truly be the last, and therefore, it was necessary to decree the absolute prohibition of all wars. This last
integral pacifism was embraced with genuine enthusiasm by
the "unofficially" revolutionary agitators, considering it one of
the most effective subversive mechanisms.

### Geneva, A Reactionary Trench

The pacifism of Geneva has become, in fact, the fortress
where all the powers that aim to banish the fatal subversive
sign weighing on this era have been accumulated. Do not forget that what is currently undergoing an essential crisis and
is principally targeted by the transmutational forces carried
by the youth is constituted by the political, social, and economic forms characteristic of the bourgeois spirit.

Indeed, the League of Nations has only ever had two objectives: first, to guarantee, as much as possible, the fulfillment
of the Treaty of Versailles by gloving the iron fist that imposed its mandates; and second, to secure the future by directly overseeing the world to prevent anyone from undermining the established status quo resulting from the victory.
These two objectives essentially merge into one: security for
France. (Although not in the sense of securing its national
integrity—that is to say, securing it from the danger of invasion—but security for France's global dominance, security for
French imperialism.)

So it is, then, that Geneva is the seat from which the most typical representative power of the forms of bourgeois civilization—that is, France—is attempting to halt the progress of the world today. All of the triumphant changes that take place in Europe, and have emerged with a certain air of service to the revolutionary spirit of the youth, have collided with Geneva. Remember the early years of Italian Fascism, the constant disconnection with Bolshevik Russia, and finally, the absolute divorce from Nazi Germany.

### *Geneva: Metropolitan Capital of French Imperialism*

The spirit and intentions that inform the League of Nations lead us to ponder whether it can be seriously considered as one of the global objectives that require more mindfulness, to guarantee the existence and security of France. Collaborating in Geneva, accepting the significance of Geneva's pacifism, essentially equates to what we've stated: causing Europe's concerns and interests to revolve around one objective, which is the security of France.

And while the right of France to exist can certainly be acknowledged, there is a substantial gap between that acknowledgement and the willingness to sacrifice everything—including justice and the historical interests of Europe—for the tranquility of France. When history shows that the normal existence of one nation becomes a bottleneck for others, one can easily imagine the fate that awaits and follows.

French imperialism is based on pacifism, to the extent that, as we have been saying, its metropolis is not Paris, but Geneva. To such an extent, the skill and artifice of the postwar system go in rescuing its own nature. This pacifist imperialism, or imperialistic pacifism, is one of those things that sustain and lives on what is contradictory to them. It is like someone getting rich and making millions by selling and spreading Bolshevik literature.

As for the pacifist tendency that we can call integral, its analysis also yields surprising results. It turns out that, adopted by apparently more revolutionary and subversive groups, it is actually a regressive, tired, and conservative attitude, its purpose marked by infantile naivety and optimism. It consists of a mindset that condemns all war and truly believes in the suppression of armed conflicts, erasing them from history. This is done in such a way that a milestone can be pointed out in the history of humanity, a moment where it can be said "up to here, nations waged war against each other; from here on, armed conflicts ceased to occur."

Indeed, it is understandable that those who believe it is so easy to completely eliminate wars also hold the belief that wars are started capriciously, by the frivolous intentions of a few rulers or a powerful trust of arms manufacturers.

### Integral Pacifism: A Weary Attitude

The integral pacifism, the one that even goes so far as to spread the belief that the homeland is not worth dying for by defending it in a war, is the ultimate flare of romantic humanitarianism, a typical flower of bourgeois civilization. How much those who are well contented with the existing order, with the withered and limping graces of the bourgeois spirit, would wish for humanitarianism as understood in this way to halt the armed force of the youthful avalanche of the era! That is why we identify the attitude of integral pacifists, those who would sacrifice everything before waging war, with a weary, disillusioned, stagnant stance: in other words, ultimately conservative and counter-revolutionary. How could they be the driving forces of a radical change, of a profound transmutation, a process that due to the resistances it would encounter could only be achieved by adopting typical wartime attitudes? This integral pacifism, this systematic avoidance of heroism and the absolute underestimation of military virtues, has triumphed and spread particularly among the workers. The first consequence has been to weaken their revolutionary strength, allowing not only them but also others to attempt to wield the highly potent subversive lever. For if war is never justified, and everything must be sacrificed to avoid it, then revolutions must also be avoided, and before making them, we must suffer through everything—unemployment, injustice, exploitation, and misery.

The pacifist position, both the one rooted in Geneva and this integral one we have mentioned, is disappearing from Europe: the former due to absolute ineffectiveness and discredit, the latter due to the vital law and the return of men to their full selves after the catastrophic abyss of 1914.

Naturally, war never appears as a desirable good. Yet it is something fatal, ingrained in the destiny of humanity, and must be accepted with fortitude, like many other terrible aspects that surround our lives. Unmasking the pacifism that has prevailed since the Great War does not equate to desiring war or being a war supporter. It equates to highlighting the contrivance and ineffectiveness of a sentiment founded on erroneous and shifting foundations. Moreover, it involves advocating, following the military conflict of 1914–1918, for men and nations to recuperate their inherent attributes of capacity for heroic sacrifice. The transmutative era we are experiencing undoubtedly demands such attributes for its full and complete realization.

## 2. Russian Bolshevism and the Global Projection of Red Subversion

### Bolshevism, Russian National Revolution

The seizure of power by Marxism in Russia is, without a doubt, the first subversive outcome of the current era, in terms of chronological order. Each passing day makes it easier to understand the true historical character of the Soviet revolution, the role to which it corresponds in the process of revolutionary achievements inaugurated after the Great War. Its legitimacy (understanding by this word its claim to present itself as a positive manifestation of the current spirit) is unquestionable. Now then, let us hasten to say that this valuable and positive contribution is valid to the extent that the deepest aspirations that guided its initial steps proved to be unsuccessful and futile.

Indeed, it could be believed, and the red instigators could naturally believe, that around 1920–21, the Soviet blaze was ready to become the sole banner of universal revolution. That is, all the transmutative capacity of our time was expected to converge and unite in the single global objective of establishing the proletarian dictatorship, in accordance with the rituals, mechanics, and purposes of Marxism. Such belief is now an absolute error, and it has no true believers even within the highest committee of the Third International. This is not because the subversive characteristics of the present historical moment have proven false, or, in other words, not because the era has become fortified or impermeable to all revolutionary endeavors, but because the Bolshevik transmutative molds have not aligned or monopolized the truly effective values of modern subversion.

The Bolshevik Revolution triumphed in Russia not so much as a strictly Marxist revolution, but rather as a national revolution. This phenomenon is not at all contradictory, and has an extremely simple explanation. In the year 1917, dur-

ing the midst of the European war, all those well-known mon-
strosities that constituted the foundation of the tsarist regime
were reaching their peak under the Russian sky. There was a
ruling aristocracy, utterly estranged from the essence of Russia, antinational in character, barely able to speak Russian
and more fluent in French, without any real understanding of
their role in Russian life. There was also a high-level bureau-
cracy that was foolish, corrupt, and that operated in an exas-
perating manner. And above all, in 1917, the crude reality of
the war's slaughter was evident, under the command of military leaders in constant conflict with victory, amidst complete
and utter disarray, with the masses blocked and punished by
every imaginable torment—hunger, despair, and powerless-
ness. Under these circumstances, the Bolsheviks were the
only ones capable of offering the salvational directives for the
situation, directives that offered nothing other than addressing the headache by cutting off the head.

Perhaps it was necessary to completely annihilate Russia
to make possible on that soil, with those large surviving Russian masses of peasants, workers, and soldiers, a national
society. The Bolsheviks were the only ones, I repeat, who
could ruthlessly wield such an annihilating lever, the only
ones who could play the required card with audacity, which
was nothing less than the definitive liquidation of historical
Russia. Their victory and triumph seem undeniable. They
played the card of Russia and they won. They incorporated
something that in this era is not only significant, but also
paramount and fruitive: a new social sense, a new way of understanding economic order, and likewise, a new conception of
the world and life. With these ingredients, they forged their
victory. But let us understand it clearly: that victory is none
other than the true construction of a fatherland. It is a national victory.

That the Soviet revolution is indeed the worldwide revolution is something that now seems to be resolved in a negative
sense. Moreover, today's Russia would not sacrifice even a

sliver of its national interests to enhance or support a revolution of its own kind in any part of the globe. It would not jeopardize its existence, the life of the Russian fatherland, nor would it compromise the social, industrial, and military structure that it has built with much pain and hope over twenty years.

Can Bolshevik Russia be considered a normal spectacle for the rest of the world? Is it not a provocation and a danger to the rest of the nations? A reactionary response to these two questions is absolutely inadmissible. From the perspective of the spirit of the era, which is to say, for those who truly feel within the reality at work in this moment of the world, Bolshevik Russia is just another nation, equipped with a social system that is more or less desirable, partly monstrous and partly intriguing to us. Does the recognition of nations as such depend on similarities in their systems and customs? Does it depend on the type of civil code they have in place?

### *The Global Bolshevik Revolution: A Failed Banner*

Now then, the notion of a universal Bolshevization must be regarded as a futile endeavor, if it ever truly materializes. The undertaking has already failed, with no possible victory. Such an aspiration belongs to the orthodox Marxist facet that accompanies Bolshevism, but as we previously mentioned, the success of Communism in Russia is not owed to the Marxist character of the revolution, but to its national character, although this turns out to be an unexpected discovery. Without the goal of forging the Russian fatherland, the regime might have possibly sunk. It has survived because it abandoned, in due time, whether voluntarily or not, the barren and erroneous elements it possessed. The defeat of Trotsky's Red Army at Warsaw marks the very moment when the European reality declared the illegitimacy of the Bolshevik Revolution as a global movement. The subsequent removal of Trotsky within

Russia itself, and the subsequent dictatorship of Stalin, corroborates this illegitimacy. Stalin may be the man who dreams of a universal red revolution, but for now, he immerses himself in Russian reality and undoubtedly believes that the most significant goal today is to create and build a great nation in Russia.

Let us reiterate that only Lenin, only a Marxist, without even blinking an eye, could lead the revolutionary strategy of October. His famous decrees following the triumph, and the tremendous decision to construct a revolutionary order through blood and fire, constitute the fundamental pillars on which the current existence of the Russian nation is built. It is becoming unquestionable whether or not Russia possesses all the ingredients and necessary mechanisms to roll through history as a fatherland for the Russians. Within Bolshevik Russia, there is a unique national discipline, a task that unifies and binds all Russians. There is a social obedience to governing hierarchies, a ruling class, a minority with a deep understanding of their guiding mission, an army that maneuvers and marches in harmony with the system, and masses that in their most lively, and consequently most potent aspect, regard this system as genuinely theirs, crafted and conceived from the ground up by them and for them. What more is needed to affirm that we are witnessing an authentic national state?

That is, considered objectively, Russia's contribution to the subversion of the era. When analyzing the significance of the events taking place in Europe, it is imperative to allocate it a place, to categorize the Soviet spectacle as one of the responses that the modern Catilinarian spirit has offered to the evident decomposition of the cultural, political, and economic forms of bourgeois liberalism.[22] Later, in Section V, we delve

---

[22] Lucius Sergius Catilina was a Roman soldier and politician who attempted to seize control of the Roman government. Catilina was defeated in the consular elections of 62 BC and assembled a revolutionary group of the disempow-

into the global Communist parties, their role within the Bolshevik phenomenon, and the worldwide Marxist actions.

### 3. *Italian Fascism: The Second Message of Subversive Youths*

#### *Fascism and Marxism, Face to Face*

The triumph of Fascism in 1922, and especially its definitive victory against all opposition in 1925, which is truly the event that establishes and consolidates it, amounts to the first response that says *"no!"* to the global Bolshevik Revolution.[23] This phenomenon holds paramount interest in understanding the exact course along which the new European forms are flowing. Well, today, thirteen years into the Fascist regime, it is naïve and certainly false to think that Mussolini gathered Italy's backward and regressive forces around the fasces to counteract and halt the Bolshevik offensive by establishing a reactionary power. This interpretation of Fascism is absolutely erroneous, and even if political parties and Marxist organizations adopt it for the sake of political battles, agitation, and revolutionary strategy, it is certain that not even the most fanatical of their leaders views and judges it in that way.

Mussolini organized and directed Fascism according to a revolutionary mystique. And what truly makes him a creator and an inventor, a modern leader, is precisely his intuition or discovery, before anyone else, of the presence in this era of a new driving force with revolutionary possibilities, or in other words, the presence of a new lever, with a different nature

---

ered—such as aristocrats who had fallen out of favor, dispossessed farmers, and indebted veterans—in order to take power by force. His attempt failed.

[23] 1922 was the year that the March on Rome occurred, a coup d'état that resulted in Mussolini and his Fascist Party ascending to power in Italy. In 1925, Tito Zaniboni, a socialist, failed in his attempt to assassinate Mussolini. As a result, Mussolini's regime enacted new laws that suppressed any oppositional political organization.

and stimulus than those traditionally accepted as such, yet capable of leading to the revolutionary conquest of the state.

Fascism is indeed the first clear proof that the Bolshevik banners not only did not exhaust or polarize all the transformational energies of the era in their defense, but, on the contrary, left out an immensely powerful and also subversive and revolutionary zone, so extensive that it would be called upon to rival Bolshevization itself in a fierce struggle, taking over the mission of dismantling the outdated system of liberal democratic forms. And to create a new order.

It was in Italy, then, that this reality became evident, where the error in the universal aims of Bolshevism was shown. Curiously, some socialist writers, not Bolshevik but still revolutionary, like the Spanish Ramos Oliveira, attribute Mussolini's victory over Marxism in Italy to "the fact that Leninism had infected the majority of Italian socialism." Perhaps these writers do not realize how profoundly insightful their observation is, not just in terms of tactical influence, but how it connects to the historical greatness of the global Bolshevik movement.

*Fascism: A Revolutionary Phenomenon*

That the Fascist phenomenon belongs to the realm of revolutionary events, nurtured by the spirit of the era, is an undeniable fact for us. What do we need to demand from a prominent political event in these times in order to place it within the revolutionary orbit, on the subversive path of serving the creative and liberating mission that befits our era? Simply the following:

1. That it contributes to the decomposition of the political and economic institutions that form the basis of the bourgeois-liberal regime, and, obviously, while avoiding granting any victory to the genuinely feudal forces.

2. By snatching the bourgeoisie of the monopoly over the helm of governance, it constructs a new national state in which the workers, the working class, collaborate in the historical mission of the Fatherland, in the destiny assigned to the whole people.

3. That it aims to subvert the current stagnation of classes by advocating a social system that bases economic equilibrium not on the framework of private gains, but on the collective interest, of the entire populace.

4. That its triumph is genuinely owed to the efforts of the newly emerging generations, maintaining a system of armed coercion as a guarantee of the revolution.

It is evident that Italian Fascism fits within these parameters, and the Fascists genuinely believe that this is the historical significance of the March on Rome. Now then, even if the level of subversion has been somewhat modest, if the concrete contribution to the social and political ascent of the workers is also limited, and if the influence of the old anti-historical powers, representative of the grand bourgeois and reactionary spirit, remains excessive, all of these, even if accepted, do not negate the revolutionary character we attribute to Fascism and allow for various explanations. One of these explanations is that every regime requires the broadest possible base from which it sustains itself, and if Fascism, having come to power after a struggle with the Marxist-oriented working class, was deprived of the necessary adherence and collaboration of large proletarian groups, it had to rely more on a different social constellation.

With Fascism, Mussolini rectified the course that the Bolsheviks were striving to establish as the only one entitled to monopolize the modern revolutionary spirit. To achieve this, the first step was to regard their approach as excessive and monstrous in its two primary and characteristic aspects: the proletarian dictatorship and the destruction of the national, which is to say, the complete political annihilation of anything that wasn't "proletarian," and equally the absolute historical annihilation of the fatherland.

Fascism was, without a doubt, willing to acknowledge the historical rationale of the proletariat, the fairness of its direct involvement as one of the sustaining forces of the new state. However, it did not agree with its singular nature, its class dictatorship against the entire nation, and certainly not with the international, anti-Italian character of the Bolshevik Revolution.

Mussolini showed through his fasci the accusation made by the reds against the "entire bourgeoisie," which is to say, against all things "extra-proletarian," as being rotten and dying remnants. In defense of Italy, to crush a revolution that he believed to be monstrous and unjust on those two fronts, he mobilized masses of combatants, drawn from various sources, many of whom came from the very sectors marked by Marxists as dying and decaying. His actions, heroic in many cases, in service not of the existing order and conservative sensibilities, but of a potential Italian revolution, asserted themselves as more robust, profound, and popular than the parallel actions carried out by Bolshevism.

Fascism revealed the presence of youth, an active mass generally drawn from the middle classes, which emerged from the struggle between classes, against the selfishness and backwardness of the bourgeoisie, and against the anti-national and exclusivist laxity of the proletariat. It turned these forces into a rectifying lever, unchained against what was truly rotten and dying within the bourgeoisie—including its decaying state apparatus, its parliamentary democracy, its exploitative manipulation of the dispossessed under the guise of freedom, its capitalist economic system, and its estrangement from Italy's patriotic and national service. Now then, this lever could not simultaneously be an anti-proletarian, anti-worker revolution. Mussolini, a former Marxist and by no means a reactionary, recognized this and had to recognize it. For him, the foremost social and political truth of the era, a truth with dire consequences for those who disregard it, was the ascent of the workers, their elevation as a fundamental pillar of the new state.

## The Economic Interests of the Masses

Consider the difficulty and fragility of a revolution like Mussolini's Fascist movement, which, despite being carried out largely against the proletarian consciousness that remained loyal to Marxism, had the historical task of raising the proletarian class to the same level of influence as the then-dominant factions of the bourgeoisie.

Given its origins and the fact that it had to confront one of the clear driving forces behind the modern upheaval that we are witnessing, Fascism shows signs of being impacted and perhaps even falling behind in fulfilling its historical mission. It is true that Fascism has effectively dismantled the political institutions of the bourgeoisie and instilled a fresh sense of morale and political optimism in the proletariat, owing to the disappearance of the old oligarchies. However, has it also managed to break down or weaken the strongholds of financial capital, the upper echelons of the industrial bourgeoisie, and the landowners, for the betterment of the overall economy and to the benefit of the broader population? Moreover, is Fascism truly progressing toward the possibility of doing away with the capitalist system and increasingly grounding the regime in the economic interests of the larger masses? It might not be enough for workers to participate in the Fascist militia and play a similar role in state politics as other classes, if the Fascist state doesn't simultaneously embrace the idea that by enhancing the economic well-being of the workers, the genuine strength of the Italian state is indeed reinforced.

Quickly we see the dangers of the revolution ultimately falling short in this aspect. Of course, this wouldn't take away from the nature of Fascism, but it would indeed highlight its historical failure, its unfinished quality, its tentative and embryonic nature. In that case, its March on Rome would evoke more the march of Sulla rather than that of Julius Caesar, and its period of leadership would resemble more a conservative and regressive phase than a revolutionary and productive one.[24]

## *The Strengthening of the State Through the Inclusion of Workers*

For the time being, the effectiveness of Fascism, in terms of having achieved proletarian collaboration, appears to be superior to that of bourgeois democracy. There is no doubt that Italian workers are currently more aligned with the Fascist state than, for instance, French workers are with the parliamentary democratic state of France. This phenomenon might stem from a sentimental situation, suggesting its transient and fluctuating nature, rather than a socio-economic reality, which would lend it a more solid value. Nevertheless, it is an existing and remarkably representative fact.

The Fascist state envisions the possibility of increasing its historical strength by making proletarian incorporation yield the same effectiveness as the incorporation of the bourgeoisie did for the Napoleonic state during the French Revolution. It is evident that Europe's astonishment at Napoleon's imperial might stemmed from the apparent lack of knowledge that the primary consequence of the revolutionary event in 1789 was to significantly fortify the state through the political rise of the bourgeoisie. This is glaringly clear to us today. Prior to 1789, the state's power was derived solely from three sources: the king, the nobility, and the Church. The French Revolution

---

[24] Lucius Cornelius Sulla Felix was a Roman general and statesman who fought a civil war, the result of which was his seizing power and becoming dictator of the Roman Republic.

placed the state on the broad and powerful shoulders of the bourgeoisie, both big and small, and Europe learned the consequences through the imperial days of Napoleon. Let us not forget that the Bonapartist spirit was essentially the Jacobin spirit manifested in hierarchy and discipline, which is to say, in a military manner.

Well then, it appears that Mussolini's perspicacity and historical-political acumen cannot escape the fact that only by achieving a similar phenomenon with the workers can he attain genuine significance for the Fascist state and a true empire for Italy.

The difficulties faced by Italian Fascism in achieving this historical perspective are enormous. We insinuated some of the more perilous challenges in what we have written. Perhaps Fascism, burdened by the problem of ensuring a strong grip from the beginning, is overly tied to old values, the persistence of which could significantly disrupt the historical ambition we have been discussing.

### Fascism and the Democratic Bourgeois Institutions

Mussolini, with a keen revolutionary spirit, dismantled the political institutions of the bourgeoisie. He dissolved the parliament, eradicated the partisan oligarchies, and shattered the myth of political freedom, all actions we do not hesitate to label as services to modern subversion. Indeed, there is nothing more unusual and disheartening than witnessing the masses granting even the slightest credibility to these political vestiges of parliamentary democracy. Their persistence not only demoralizes and corrupts the labor parties but also guarantees victory to the bourgeoisie, who control the wealth and thereby monopolize extensive propaganda, the press, and all mechanisms of electoral success.

Indeed, the Fascist revolution boasts both the practical and theoretical dismantling of democratic-bourgeois political forms. And though this may be perceived by the global Marxist sector as an invigoration of bourgeois positions, as it reinforces their security with institutions more robust than parliamentary ones, the historical consequences that, in our opinion, should be inferred from this fact are precisely of the opposite nature, because once the bourgeoisie is displaced from the political forms and institutions that are uniquely its creation and upon which its economic development and social strength inherently rely, it becomes evident that it is ultimately weakened as a historical and political force.

To snatch from the bourgeoisie in a country their parliamentary democracy, their reverence for the free economic and political play of individualistic energies, and to do so definitively, systematically, and doctrinally—which is to say, not in the style of transient reactionary dictatorships, the kind that leave room for the future and that the good bourgeois certainly applauds, as was the case here in Spain with General Primo de Rivera—to take all of that away in the manner that Fascism does, with a certain Catilinarian flavor and public devotion to the myths of empire, direct action, and absolute coercion, is undoubtedly to initiate the radical decomposition of the bourgeoisie as the ruling and predominant class. In short, the bourgeois spirit, which we will address in a subsequent chapter, does not thrive in the atmosphere of Fascism; it is not present within it, nor does it move within its ranks like a fish in water or a lion in the jungle. It is not in its element. This leads us to draw a conclusion: Fascism is not a creation of the bourgeoisie, nor a product of its mindset, culture, or even its way of life.

Perhaps with Fascism, as we previously hinted in relation to the Soviet regime, a similar situation arises. They are both typical phenomena of the rebellion beginning to unfold in our era, characterized by aspects that are neither definitive nor conclusive. Instead, they resemble the initial eruptions that herald something yet to come, which is why contradictions abound within them: contradictions never seen in finalized, complete, and perfect systems. Hence, we find the paradox that Marxism, an international doctrine that has no allegiance to the concept of the fatherland, somehow saves Russia "nationally," a phenomenon perhaps as strange as an almond tree sprouting where an orange tree was planted. Similarly, Italian Fascism, victorious against the proletarians—and that in many aspects, finance not being the least of which—and supported by the grand bourgeoisie, has to be the one seeking to strengthen its state through the allegiance and collaboration of the workers.

## 4. Socialist Racism in Germany

Here is another significant phenomenon of modern subversion that has grown and triumphed, not only outside the Bolshevik sphere, but in opposition to it. Now then, to comprehend it accurately, the first requirement is to strip it of the "Fascist" label. For none of the essential values, none of the substantive ingredients that characterize the National Socialist movement and that can be identified as determinants of its victory, progenerate from Italian Fascism. The form of the salute, the uniform of its masses, and the rigid discipline under a leader are truly superficial and episodic aspects of it, lacking any substantial significance as the backbone of its revolution.

### What Is the "National"?

Once again, as with the ultimate consequences of Bolshevism, as with one of the fundamental categories of Fascism, we find ourselves here facing a "national" phenomenon, something that occurs within the realm of the "national," and being inside of it, it is justified in its entirety. But of course it is crucial to clarify this expression, for the significance of the national varies significantly for a Russian Bolshevik, an Italian Fascist, and a German social-racist.

In the Russian Bolshevik's perspective, the national is an unexpected discovery, a value that suddenly emerges on the historical path of their revolution, a consequence that truly shapes their endeavor and is undoubtedly embraced with genuine jubilation.

In the Italian Fascist's perspective, the national becomes a turbine generating enthusiasm, an ideal necessity without which one feels degraded, reduced to historical vileness. It is a blend of dream, fantasy, and myth.

The German National Socialist perceives this concept as a metaphysical anguish, operating on a biological and profound mechanism: blood. Hence, it is inherently racist. For them, then, Germany is a living organism, progressing through history in a state of turmoil, a combination of distress and strength, always sustained by the spirit of sacrifice and the very vitality of all Germans.

## The National Socialist Synthesis

The synthesis of the national and the social, which appears to foreign observers and commentators as the supreme difficulty conquered by Adolf Hitler, is illuminated in the light of socialist racism as an astonishingly simple endeavor. The agitation surrounding issues of social-economic nature, the task of addressing their crises and delineating to the masses the very disorders and harms that befall them, seems exceedingly dry in other nations, with the only possible emotion being, if anything, of a negative kind based on demagogic promises that cater to the specific desires of large audiences. However, in Germany, a fundamental variant arises, marked by clear racist undertones, and its handling has indeed secured Hitler's victory. For the misfortune of each German is not solely their own; it coincides and identifies with the misfortune of Germany as a whole, of the entire Fatherland.

Hitler, in his fervent speeches before massive gatherings of Germans, depicted the dire scenario the German people confronted, a nation in ruins, with forced unemployment, the constant specter of genuine economic servitude, and a sense of disgrace. It was within these fervent speeches that his most resounding successes and deepest emotional bonds with the masses emerged. By deducing the consequences that these hardships would inflict upon Germany, he forged a powerful connection that resonated deeply. Therefore, he highlighted how it was imperative, essential, and urgent to restore bread and prosperity to the Germans, in order to make a great Germany possible once again. Of course, this sort of appeal to the German fatherland also permitted Hitler to simultaneously point out to the vast masses that the originators and culprits of their material misfortunes were not some erroneous ideas or mere abstractions, but rather concrete enemies, enemies of Germany itself as a nation, and above all, these enemies were clearly visible and identifiable, easily pointed out by hand: on one hand, the Jews and their financial capital; on the other, Germany's external enemy, Versailles, and its negotiators, signatories, and maintainers, which is to say, the Marxists and the bourgeoisie of the Weimar Republic.

The German people grasped and truly understood the voice of Hitler, which spoke to the deepest and most profound aspects of their nature. He sublimated their daily anxieties, giving them a heroic significance and the supreme categorization of a German national catastrophe. In this way, the forcibly unemployed worker, the bankrupt industrialist, the soldier without a flag, the student lacking warmth, the former landowner without fortune, the entire large mass of people discarded and neglected by the existing system, began to comprehend that all their miseries and disquiet were the product of a great crime committed against Germany. This crime was hidden from the people by the cowardice and treachery of the

"November Criminals," the architects of the Weimar regime and true accomplices in all acts perpetrated against Germany.[25] These parties and factions constituted groups whose spirit was entirely foreign to the spirit of Germany. They were manipulated by the Jews and devised by individuals of other races, invaders and annihilators of the great German race.

Thus, the Germans commenced to uplift their spirit, to overcome, and to "awaken." *"Deutschland, erwache!"* ("Germany, awake!") was the resounding and constant cry of the Nazis. For there is no more effective medicine, no surer resource to restore vigor to a disregarded and afflicted nation, than to point out with a firm finger the powers and forces responsible for their neglect, their anguish, and their misery.

### *Not a Socialism for Man, but for the German*

The emotional complex driving socialist racism is quite simple. We are in the presence of a social idea, a socialism, whose motivation lies not in the need to achieve justice for Germans as individuals suffering from an unjust economic system, but rather in the notion of attaining the best and fairest social system for Germany as a nation, a race, a living entity.

That is why Hitler's anti-capitalism differs from Marxist anti-capitalism. The former does not merely view the capitalist system as a specific set of economic relations, but also sees the Jew; it adds a racial element to the strict economic concept. The anti-Jewish idea and the anti-capitalist idea are merely the same for National Socialism. As we have mentioned, the German individualizes his particular issue within Germany, and his socialist concerns consistently pursue an arrangement for the benefit of the entire race.

---

[25] Those German politicians who signed the Treaty of Versailles in November of 1918 are sometimes called the November Criminals by their detractors.

Marxism, therefore, left the German's most intimate and vigorous reactions untouched. It occasionally slid across his surface, and only in the false Germans, which is to say, those individuals naturalized in Germany yet estranged from the voice of blood, from the myth of race, could it constitute a more profound stance.

It is not, therefore, "man," but the *German*, who becomes the esteemed object for racist socialism, which is why Hitler's program distinctly outlines differences between those he labels "German citizens" and others, the rest who may reside in Germany as foreigners, claiming the right to participate in Germany's economic wealth and opportunities solely for the former group.

## In Service of Subversion

The Hitlerian movement immediately polarized the subversive potential of the youth around its swastika. This fact, this detail, is what makes it a modern phenomenon, situated on the transformational line, and reinforces its revolutionary value in the ongoing global process.

Its victory has also occurred before the astonished eyes of the traditional "revolutionaries." Ten or twelve million Marxists have been witnesses from up close, observing with rapid blinks of astonishment the spectacle of Catilinarian masses vying for control, without needing anything from Marxism, bypassing it in their ascending and rectifying strategy: a typical phenomenon of rivalry, in which one revolution triumphs over another by seizing power first.

Who can doubt that the Hitlerist masses, those people in brown uniforms with youth on their shoulders, were more revolutionary and subversive than the others, the well-behaved social democrats, encased in their unions and exuding prudence and years from every pore? The former were the true dissenters, the true mobilized forces for the transformative task; they were the ones truly equipped with the energy and determination needed to confront Germany's challenges.

The episode of Hitler's seizure of power, as well as the subsequent process and events that allowed him to be the sole and supreme leader of the Reich, also carries the mark of something fateful, direct, and certain, something whose evasion and concealment are in vain and impossible. All resistances and challenges were mobilized to halt the march of National Socialism, to dismantle its forces, and to undermine its revolutionary distinctiveness at a crucial hour. Nothing proved to be of any use. For the mechanics of Hitlerism controlled the essential driving forces and swept away everything with the firmest stride and the blindest faith. He seized power in the most suitable, straightforward, and natural manner, as befits a strategist who understands the secret of these times: the distinction between the issue of acquiring or conquering power and the revolutionary challenge, which involves conducting a revolution, a highly serious and complex undertaking that requires time and must be strategically detached from the former.

### After the Marxist Wall, the Other Two: The Military Oligarchy and the Junkers

Hitler assumed power, not without immense challenges, not without testing his faith in the ultimate destinies of National Socialism, not without being obligated to negotiate concessions, and even almost tolerating his entry into the chancellorship while muzzled by the Junkers.

The Junkers, the nobility, were the ones who executed the final tactical maneuver to impede the National Socialist revolution. They opened the doors of the chancellorship to Hitler, thinking he was already subdued and ready to drown the revolution himself, to adopt a policy inspired by the traditional, Prussian, and reactionary line of the Junkers, and to remain indifferent and silent in the face of the subversive desires of the Nazi masses.

It is known how General von Schleicher, hours before Hitler's rise to power, organized a military coup with the garrisons of Berlin's cantonments and sought the support of the social democratic unions to flank him with a general strike. The hesitation of these elements, who were not inclined toward revolutions or ventures, allowed the Junkers' plan to be executed: forming a government under Hitler's leadership in which he would not attain the majority. Hitler made all the concessions requested of him, accepted the minimal representation of two ministers, was willing to cover up the controversial issue of "aid to the East," and so forth. However, Hitler knew well that victory was essentially already his. After leaving behind the defeated mass of Marxism and diminishing Schleicher's military power, the struggle with those Junkers, those small audacious groups without any vigor, seemed like mere child's play to him. If they inspired any respect, it was because behind the Junkers, the old Marshal Hindenburg still lived on in the presidency of the Reich.[26]

The two or three months of collaboration and conflict with the "nobility" constitute the most fascinating scene in terms of the overpowering force of National Socialism. It is evident how events effortlessly fall into place for him, even at the cost of visible confrontations that struck fear into the hearts of the Junkers. These clear signs indicated to him with an extremely eloquent gesture the complete and radical loss of the battle.

To what extent will the German national revolution be realized, and what destiny awaits it? The days of retribution in June 1934 showcased its tremendous pathos and drama.[27] It was during those days that Strasser, the National Socialist most aligned with the genuine interests of the broad popular

---

[26] Kurt Ferdinand Friedrich Hermann von Schleicher was a German general and a chancellor of Germany in the Weimar Republic. He became a political rival to Hitler, which resulted in his assassination during the Night of the Long Knives.

[27] This date refers to the previously mentioned Night of the Long Knives.

masses, perished, and it was during those days that the specter of disillusionment and discouragement first appeared before the youth.[28] Everything seems to be conjured now, and
with Hitler at the helm of Germany's destiny, at the helm of
seventy million Germans, escorted by the twin ideals of race
and blood, he is and remains, regardless of his eventual fate,
one of the most moving, extraordinary, and surprising phenomena in world history.

There remains another notable response, another grand
manifestation of the colossal revolutionary spirit that currently operates with global jurisdiction.

## 5. The Impotence or Revolutionary Incapacity of Marxism

In the sections dedicated to Italian Fascism and German
socialist racism, we have already insinuated and outlined this
fact. It is not readily accepted, and least of all by Marxists,
that in this era of clear subversive tendencies, Marxism, as a
revolutionary doctrine and revolutionary banner, may not be
the one interpreting and guiding the changes occurring in Europe. For at the very dawn of this era, when the subversive
events commenced with Russian Bolshevism, Marxism appeared to harness all revolutionary energies and, owing to its
own prestige and significance among the proletariat, seemed
poised to successfully effect the economic and political transformations that were foreseen.

Now, then, since it has not been and has not turned out
that way, it does not seem to us at this point in May 1935 a
theoretical or speculative assertion, but a factual affirmation
based on the undeniable events that have been unfolding.

Nevertheless, despite this, Marxism has perhaps been the
most fertile political-social movement for the past century and

---

[28] Gregor Strasser was an early leader of the Nazi Party. He held many left-
wing views, which brought him into conflict with Hitler. He, too, was purged
during the Night of the Long Knives.

a half, since the French Revolution, and one among the five or six most significant of the entire last millennium. However, Marxism is rapidly moving away from triumphant stages, and remains outside the transmutations that are taking place, even when these transformations are clearly imbued with a social character. It pursues, as one of its most valuable objectives, the ascension of the proletariat to the status of pillars and sustainers of the state.

We do not believe that the revolutionary incapacity of Marxism is unrelated to the presence of several factors that accompany, limit, and define its boundaries, leaving numerous forces outside its walls, forces that are equally dissatisfied and not accountable for the capitalist economic system. These forces possess a significant capacity for enthusiasm, political struggle, and the exploration of new social and political forms.

Those factors are clearly:

## The Triumph of Bolshevism in Russia

The worldwide Marxist front has indeed been paradoxically fractured by the Soviet victory. And this is not only due to the immediate consequence of dividing it into two factions, two internationals, and two banners. It is because of something more profound and with more serious consequences. Since 1921, a date we can point to as the end of war Communism and the civil war against the counter-revolutionary White armies, as well as the beginning of a more "normal" construction of socialist economy in Russia, the subversive influence of the Soviet revolution debilitates and diminishes in other nations.

Evidently, the red armies in the field were more effective for Marxist propaganda than films about electrification, graphic magazines with bronze busts of proletarians, and the regime's large public works. The Bolshevik hour was that: the Bolshevism of war. Lenin saw this with absolute clarity. The famous Twenty-one Conditions, dictated by him as a definition of what the Third International was and had to be, aimed to connect the global Bolshevik Revolution with the heroic and "ascendant" periods of the Russian revolution.[29] In the third condition, it declared that in Europe and America, "the class struggle is now fully entering the period of civil war." However, it happened that the Russian Revolution stood as the sole triumph; the Hungarian Bolsheviks failed, the German Bolsheviks failed, and, as it inevitably had to occur, the Third International based in Moscow completely lost touch with reality, issuing slogans that often took on a truly picturesque character. In essence, it was reduced to being a "Bolshevik fatherland for Russians" once Russia alone emerged as victorious. It became an organization for propaganda and espionage, serving Moscow's imperialism and interests.

The global Communist parties quickly demonstrated their impotence for the revolutionary conquest of power, and where they temporarily seized it, as in Hungary and Bavaria, they showed an inability to retain it and establish a socialist regime. This shattered the militant foundation on which Marxism relied, as the Communist ranks were, indeed, the revolutionary phalanx of the worldwide Marxist movement.

In such a scenario, the Bolshevik groups, growing more confrontational and at odds with the middle classes rising to a level of "social revolutionary awareness," have fulfilled no other mission than that of highly effective "provocateurs," triggering the triumph of Fascism in Italy and Hitler's racism in Germany. Nothing more.

The triumphant Russian revolution also divorced Marxism from its creative myth, its hope for something truly new that would channel the illusions of the masses toward entirely uncharted objectives. It is not the same to frivolously stage a revolution "to establish what exists in another country," such

---

[29] The Twenty-one Conditions were twenty-one points, mostly created by Vladimir Lenin, to which socialist parties in the Third International were supposed to adhere.

as the Russian regime, as it is to undertake one driven by a radically subversive and dissatisfied consciousness, a genuine product of the immediate realities upon which revolutions always operate.

And what about non-Bolshevik Marxism? What about the socialist parties? Indeed, European events indicate that they have suffered nearly the same fate as the Communist parties. Their distancing and detachment from them did not provide the advantages that were expected: the absorption of other elements and the broadening of their base by capturing the subversive aspirations of the entire youth and the non-proletarianized middle classes, who were nonetheless crushed and sunken by large financial capital. In general, the socialist parties and organizations were not "a distinct revolutionary strategy" from that of Bolshevism; rather, they often represented a renunciation of any revolutionary strategy. As a result, if they managed to expand their base somewhat, it was due to the sympathy this stance found among more liberal sectors of bourgeois society, those leaning more toward counter-revolution and ineffectiveness. The rectifications they attempted have also been unfortunate, as was evident in February 1934 in Austria and the following October in Spain.

### The Slogan of Class Exclusivity: The Dictatorship of the Proletariat

Here is another factor that should not be forgotten. Marxist dogmatism, due to excessive fidelity to the letter, has perhaps rendered one of its most fertile postulates ineffective: its character as a doctrine in service of the workers, the proletarians, and its formidable tendency to turn them into a positive historical force. As we have expressed earlier, this involves the "incorporation of workers into political and social tasks of guiding and leading character." However, Marxism rigidly stretched this same purpose to the limit with the well-known slogan of the dictatorship of the proletariat, thus decreeing non-collaboration and the disappearance of all revolutionary values that do not conform to a class-oriented perspective.

Thus, Marxism excluded a vast social zone, composed precisely of people who were products of the newest economic forms. These were individuals with a difficult classification because they did not represent any particular capitalist interest, and yet did not fit among the wage workers, either. This includes small industrialists without capital, office workers of large enterprises, the entire university youth, and small landowning cultivators. It was not possible for these social segments to simply accept being enlisted under a slogan as closed, hermetic, and rigorous as the Marxist dictum of proletarian dictatorship. Moreover, this entire zone of people is increasing in numerical strength each day and is also assuming, even more than the wage workers, the role of victims of the crises and vicissitudes that the capitalist system is going through. Marxism has prevented them from identifying their struggle with that of the proletariat, which is why, together with nationalist intellectuals, they have adopted a subversive, battle-oriented style; they have forged a different path. In Italy, this gave rise to Fascism; in Germany, to socialist racism; and in other regions, they continue without a clear direction, or, as in Spain, provide electoral victories to capitalist and bourgeois right-wing parties, such as the occurrence of November 1933.

The slogan of the dictatorship of the proletariat is also strategically naive. It begins, without gaining any benefit from it, by preempting the entire process of revolution and presenting proletarian power as the primary objective. The bourgeois revolution, the French Revolution, which Marxism dialectically explains as its historical antecedent, was not carried out by the bourgeoisie with an exclusive class consciousness. In other words, it didn't unfold under the banner of "all power to the bourgeoisie!" even though that consequence eventually came to be. Instead, it advocated for political and social reforms that, naturally, once imposed and established or in the process of being so, eventually placed full power in the hands of the bourgeoisie.

### Its Ignorance of the National

Here we have another factor, another great fortress which Marxism can neither perceive nor overcome. After the war, after ten million men died defending their fatherlands, the idea of the nation revealed itself as one of the deepest dimensions shaping man's social life. Marxist internationalism declared the national to be outside of any revolutionary emotion, thus depriving itself of one of the great levers of subversion. This vacuum was quickly seized upon in Europe and adopted as a salvation slogan by large crowds. The idea of the fatherland and the defense of the fatherland are indeed obvious labels of political reaction. Often, when invoked by regressive factions, they are used to shield their economic privileges. However, all of this only underscores the strength of the steel of that shield: the effectiveness of the national idea as a stronghold. Instead of revolutionaries' desire to deny the fatherland, or even deny its existence, this should have sparked the contrary desire to conquer it for the revolution.

### Marxism Underestimates Revolutionary Values of Maximum Effectiveness

It seems evident that Marxism has not succeeded in harnessing all the emotional, formal, and practical levers that exist in the present era for its revolutionary action. Its subversive drive, its revolutionary struggle for power, has lacked success. Its strategy is tailored for a conflict with the liberal democratic systems, and is even influenced by a somewhat optimistic belief that its hour, within the course of historical succession, will arrive without the need for significant up-heavals.

Thus, the mechanism of the general strike, the adoption of positions rooted in anti-militarism and anti-heroism, the gradual intellectualization of workers, and so on, which were effective revolutionary tools within a limited radius, proved insufficient and mediocre as the transmutative era unfolded. These strategies were effective against a society with limited upheavals, such as parliamentary democracy, but they fell short as the times underwent significant change.

In the presence of rival revolutionary forces and as a re-flection of the Bolshevik years during the era of war Com-munism, Marxist organizations began making adjustments to their strategic plans. They introduced a certain sense of mili-tary ethos, called for discipline, and stressed the need to ac-quire military-style efficiency. However, the results were not particularly satisfying. After all, Marxism had traditionally been devoted to discrediting and eradicating any qualities associated with that type of ethos, any human tendency to-ward a military-style discipline that it derogatorily referred to as "barracks-like," and in a comprehensive manner, informed by a humanitarian pacifism that disregarded the soldierly qualities of humanity, a stance with an unmistakable bour-geois hue. It is understandable that Marxism, like any revolu-tionary organization, would be anti-militaristic in respect to the enemy state, striving to prevent it from bolstering its armed base since the aim is to overcome it. However, this is vastly different from renouncing within one's own revolution-ary ranks the unique values of military discipline, the ethos of the military, and even renouncing the heroic myths and the creative illusion of conquest and dominance.

Again, in Marxism, the destiny of Catiline is fulfilled; he paid for his military incapacity with defeat, his lack of skill in transforming subversive masses into powerful armies. Cati-line, who can be considered chronologically as the first revolu-tionary in history, launched his action at an exact juncture in

Rome, but his character was more that of an agitator and intellectual rather than a military leader. It was solely for this reason that his revolution was defeated. The evidence lies in the fact that a few years later, Julius Caesar, with the same program as Catiline, yet possessing remarkable military virtues and qualities, achieved victory.

Today it can be asserted without a doubt that if the large masses of proletarians, mobilized by Marxism in this era, had achieved military efficiency, it might have been impossible to deny them victory.

Thus it happens that Marxism encounters insurmountable difficulties in the conquest of power. Nevertheless, it is confident in its ability to solidify itself and triumphantly build a new economic system if it were to achieve that conquest successfully. We have heard the same phrase from two prominent Marxists, one Spanish and the other French, which points out and highlights the current dilemma of Marxism: "Give us the power," they said, "and you will see how we sustain ourselves in it while actualizing socialism." Their problem is the problem of power—no other—which is precisely the unavoidable problem if it hopes to play any role in the contemporary transformation, because there are other forces pursuing the same quarry.[30]

### 6. The Demolition of Liberalism. Decrepitude of the Political and Economic Forms of the Individualistic Bourgeoisie

Nothing is more contrary to the mindset, needs, and significance of our era than the political and economic forms devised by the liberal-bourgeois spirit. These forms have outlived their own effectiveness, and people are now casting

---

[30] After the Bolshevik Revolution, all insurrectional attempts of Marxist nature have failed. Here are some examples, not counting those that followed immediately after the aforementioned one: Hamburg Insurrection (1923), Estonia (1924), China (1926 and 1927), Austria (1934), and Spain (1934).

them aside as tools whose use has become ruinous and irritating. The revolt whose development is being outlined in these pages truly acts as a liberator from those old forms, and constitutes an endeavor to break free from them, to escape their expiration.

The persistence and longevity of the liberal democratic institutions would, in today's world, signify the impossibility of extracting any value from this era, condemning it to live imprisoned by forms that are alien to it, in a state of amputation and paralysis.

It is noteworthy, however, that the current era manages, in a relatively simple manner, to successfully rid itself of the danger of distortion and annulment. This is evidenced by the subversive reality we have been studying, which is populated, as it has been shown, not with failures or unsuccessful attempts, but with resounding and complete victories.

The outcome of the contemporary transmutation will inevitably be the defeat of all political, economic, and cultural forms inherent to the mindset and spirit of the capitalist bourgeoisie. Simultaneously, these forms will be replaced by others that are a direct creation of the forces currently representative and active.

If we analyze the vital and social characteristics of the bourgeois spirit a little, we will quickly perceive its absolute opposition and radical contradiction with the most vibrant and fertile values that are emerging today.

## *Its Individualistic Attitude*

The democratic-bourgeois institutions have been developed under the belief that the individual, as such, is the creative subject of history, and therefore that the pursuit of one's own goals as an individual is the most respectable and fruitful mission of humanity. Everything must be sacrificed to this individual mission, starting with the state, which not only should not hinder or mediate it, but must effectively guarantee it. This is the marrow of the liberal state, the function and purpose ascribed to it by the bourgeoisie.

The liberal state is merely a tool for the individual. It must not undermine the freedom of the individual in any way, nor sacrifice that freedom for any other value. Its coercive apparatus is justified in terms of freedom, and it guarantees the freedom and "rights" of individuals.

It is noteworthy that such institutions made it possible for the historical strengthening of the capitalist system, the culmination of a social class, the bourgeoisie, which maximized the creative energy of its members and propelled significant economic, cultural, and political progress. During this period, the individual achieved remarkable gains, acquired immense social influence, and also attained a very high standard of living. Everything was at his service, within reach, to be used as an instrument of power, wisdom, or wealth.

The significant importance of that historical phase and the valuable gains humanity made during it cannot be denied. What can be affirmed, however, is that its period of validity has been short, and today we clearly see the bundle of contradictions and abnormalities it contained. No matter how modest one's powers of observation and understanding may be, anyone can perceive and understand them today (or at least sense them, which is equally valid).

It soon became evident that the supposed individual greatness and generosity that informed those institutions were in fact accessible to very few, and they existed and persisted at the expense of atrocious injustices.

And it was accessible to very few, not because there were few outstanding individuals, but due to the inherent nature of the system and the goals deemed desirable. There were many men who could aspire to political power, wealth, and culture, with talents and abilities to attain them, yet inevitably, this trinity of goods had to be hoarded and monopolized by the very few. However, since the system allowed and facilitated competition, struggle, and contention, people engaged in them with frenzy.

And there we have the turbines that operated within the heart of bourgeois individualism: political parties, in increasing numbers and abundance, with distinct programmatic aspirations and ideals, economic enterprises, production without order or concert, financial speculation, various schools and morals, and the spiritual disintegration of culture.

## Diminishment of Man

And here is how the bourgeois spirit, in the name of honoring and exalting the individual dimension of man, led him to contradictions and outcomes like those we witness today—of course, not without passing through stages of certain splendor and liberating humanity from abominable regressive powers. Political liberalism and economic capitalism now seem to us entities and forms brimming with vacancy, inefficacy, and injustice. But they have fulfilled a historical mission, all the more recognized as such by their current challengers, who, with haste and vigor, declare them false and obsolete. The evidence lies in the fact that the subversion is not carried out by the political powers displaced by liberal bourgeoisie, which is to say, the *ancien régime*, despite still being defended and upheld by some. Similarly, the overthrow of capitalism is not attempted by the economic and social forms that preceded it.

The contemporary subversion, in burying the bourgeois capitalist liberal democratic forms, does so revolutionarily, meaning it does not revert to old forms, but rather discovers and invents new ones.

Eventually, amidst the institutions of liberal-bourgeois civilization, man emerged mistreated, exploited, and diminished.

Political freedom inevitably crystallized into parliamentary democracy, and this system swiftly transferred power to party oligarchies, to magnates who controlled electoral mechanisms, the major press outlets, and expensive propaganda.

Economic freedom often reduced the individual man to a mere commodity in the majority of cases, if not to the dreadful status of unemployment, a social residue.

Ultimately, man was deprived of permanent and secure values: all those that originate and find their meaning in extra-individual human spheres—the values of community, of militancy, of just discipline, and the value of the fatherland, the national dimension of man, one that begins before him and continues after him. I do not mention the religious value, as this has not been truly endangered under the banner of the individualistic bourgeoisie, since among individual goals, religious concerns of saving the soul fit perfectly.

In summary, the prevalence of distinctly bourgeois ways of life exclusively led to the elevation of a political minority (the oligarchs) and a social minority (the major capitalists), and as this situation of privilege lacked and still lacks profound roots, in other words, it is not founded on hierarchically recognized values of justice, but rather stems from free competition and can be aspired to by all, suspicion arises that they might be the result of deceit, falsehood, and injustice, making them all the more irritating and insufferable.

### The Discontented Vanguard

Naturally, it was the workers who were the first to perceive that the political and economic world created by bourgeois liberal democracy was, in fact, quite uninhabitable and artificial. Their historic response was Marxism, the first systematic challenge and the initial obstacle encountered on the path of parliamentary democracy. It is evident that the liberal democratic system finds its practical and theoretical justification only when considered by all as an acceptable method of coexistence. However, Marxism decreed and achieved a rupture of solidarity between the proletarians and other classes, furnishing workers with a doctrine and a flag that left no room for peaceful and legal collaboration with them. Despite other interpretations of Marxism, it seems to contain a powerful and immensely fertile inclination to distance workers not only from the bourgeois myth of liberal democracy, but even from the very myth of political freedom. Lenin's question, "Freedom, for what?" is even more profound than believed, spoken by a Marxist, and its response is truly challenging in this critical hour of world politics.

### *Exhaustion and Contemplation of One's Own Ruins*

It is well-known that one of the political achievements being pursued today in Europe is the displacement of the bourgeois spirit from the governing realms. Parliamentary democracy granted and will continue to grant power to the bourgeoisie itself, or its most direct representatives, which are the political parties.

But it so happens that the bourgeois individual is completely lacking in the capacity for guiding political tasks. He is the social type least suited for the exercise of political power. He entirely lacks the sense of the collective, the spirit of the popular community, historical ambition, and a heroic spirit.

Everything that is now acting as a germ of fragmentation, impotence, weariness, and selfishness is directly due to the social dominance of the bourgeoisie and the political dominance of its agents, lawyers, and figureheads.

The democratic-bourgeois civilization has entered a final stage, characterized by hypocrisy, as it has lost faith in its own principles and now seeks to sustain itself by cynically distorting and falsifying them. This endeavor is facilitated by the fact that the characteristic attitude of the democratic-bourgeois spirit—its tendency toward criticism, blindness to the collective, lukewarm patriotism, false sentimental humanitarianism, and so forth—is shared by wide and extensive segments of society, extending beyond layers and sectors of economic privilege to encompass even popular and proletarian groups, influenced by its more vile and degraded characteristics.

But this historical attitude, in its most representative and active sector, now fully recognizes its infertility and exhaustion. It realizes that its political ideals, far from building and constructing anything, transform into sources of destruction and discord as soon as they leave their lips. It knows that its system and economic arrangement lead to the advent of colossal crises, to its own downfall, and to the hunger of the large masses in forced unemployment. It also sees that the political and social institutions it has created turn nations into permanent theaters of bloody conflicts, steadily weakening national solidarity to the point of jeopardizing the very historical existence of peoples. It acknowledges its inability to know what to do with the vast waves of youth that keep arriving, and ultimately contemplates the imminent exhaustion and irreparable disappearance that lie ahead.

## 7. Forced Unemployment. Humanity Exposed to the Elements

The entire current economy is based on and built at the expense of an astonishingly simple mechanism, whose sole purpose is this: human enrichment. Since the late eighteenth century, when an unforeseen and astounding event like industrial mechanization occurred, certain individuals have had at their disposal increasingly fertile and wondrous means to achieve this goal with remarkable speed. The human population grew in considerable proportions, and its presence was welcomed with utmost joy, for it served a dual and crucial function, which was then and has been until now essential:

the dual function of producing and consuming, both on a co-lossal and frenzied scale.

It matters little to point out whether the enormous increase in the human population was due to the life forms, radiant and splendid, that emerged in the world with mechanized civilization and large industrial enterprises, or whether, on the contrary, these were purely effects of global overpopulation. The fact is that both phenomena coincide and interlock in such a way that they bring about identical consequences.

With great ease, one can trace minute by minute the process we refer to, from the day, for example, when the first textile factories were set up in England, up to the very day we are writing, thus witnessing the complete development of the capitalist system. The trajectory would comprise, then, the pioneers who applied the initial advantages of mechanization to manufacturing goods, to the current manifestations of industrial trusts and major sales crises, moving from the emergence of a small minority of "free" manufacturers with limited resources and fledgling machinery, to the zenith of financial capital, costly large-scale equipment, and joint-stock companies. The precise examination of this significant trajectory may not concern us; instead, our focus lies on its social aspect, particularly insofar as it explains the meaning of forced unemployment and the current misery of the masses.

## The Ideal of Progressive Enrichment

There have always been people throughout history dedicated to increasing their wealth as much as possible, but the truth is that experience had shown most people that becoming rich was only possible on relatively few occasions. That is why, until the late eighteenth century, the majority of people lived without a tendency to become rich, directing their capabilities toward tasks that provided a different type of satisfaction than the accumulation and concentration of capital. Additionally, conditions naturally were such that the possibilities of wealth creation were, so to speak, obscured. The realm of what we now call "business" was limited. Existing fortunes had a feudal character, and the families owning them, generally belonging to the nobility, were far from entrusting their money to any kind of financial speculators. On the other hand, the guilds were almost static economic forms, having very little inclination toward adventure.

The emergence of mechanization had as its first consequence an absolute change in the landscape. People now had numerous means to enrich themselves quickly. The matter was quite simple. The discovery had been made of things, the machines, which produced highly sought-after goods, by cost-effective means.

The discovery of mechanical means of producing goods was followed by the discovery of ways to transport them everywhere, delivering them to consumption centers with utmost convenience and in minimal time. The economic result was splendid. Everyone could venture toward newly emerging industrial and commercial gold. There was room for all those arriving because, apart from the fact that the world voraciously consumed all products, there was also the possibility, thanks to technical advancements and inventive genius, to outcompete rival manufacturers by seizing markets when danger of depletion arose. This was achieved through the use of more perfect machinery, more efficient production rationalization, and the equally efficient organization of transportation.

In such a situation, it seemed practically impossible for the industrial process to come to a halt, because difficulties could always be overcome, either by conquering new markets, or by using better and faster machinery.

What interests us here is to highlight, in a couple of paragraphs, the immediate consequences of the growing frenzy of production that gripped the human sector in control of the industrial apparatus. Thousands of new industries emerged;

their equipment was constantly renewed, introducing reforms that always aimed to produce more and more in less time. As industrial technology advanced, it naturally required more powerful financial means to establish large factories. On one hand, machinery became more expensive due to its increasing complexity and perfection; on the other hand, vertical organization of production was imposed to surpass cost conditions and gain an advantage over free competition.

The substantial profits acquired by the industrialists were converted into financial capital, which was then used by the new enterprises, which the development of production necessitated. Existing industries were expanded, and the acquisition of increasingly costly equipment became essential. However, the available financial capital proved insufficient. Consequently, large joint-stock companies and banking institutions were expanded, gathering savings and financial resources from numerous private fortunes, including those newly amassed during the industrialization process as well as those older static fortunes tied to land.

Everything entered into the service of global production. The ideal of amassing wealth became increasingly prevalent. New businesses and the significant expansion of existing ones continued to require tremendous financial resources. These resources were obtained through various forms of speculation and credit manipulation. Only by achieving incessant and ongoing success, meaning producing more and in better conditions each day, could the immense speculative apparatus that hovered over the global production network be sustained.

Such an economic system, based on limitless production and relying on increasingly tightening financial and human conditions brought about by mechanization, carries tremendous contradictions. For the moment even the slightest hint of a crisis or a mandatory decrease in production arises for a major industry, it would find itself, having prepared for the opposite scenario, namely, further increasing output, facing a situation where a reduction would undermine its very foundations of existence. The large industry, therefore, is not free to regulate production.

For instance, fifty years ago, if any industrial sector needed to reduce its production pace by 20 percent, it was a feasible task without serious disruptions, as a variable number of workers could be withdrawn and shifted to other jobs or different industries. However, today, such a phenomenon takes on immediate catastrophic proportions. Firstly, because the dismissed workers have no other employment options, and secondly, because it would cast an even deeper threat on the economic life, aside from the extreme distress of unemployment: the danger of halting the machinery. The shutdown of large-scale machinery, the costly equipment of major industries, poses a calamity of such magnitude that it vertically undermines the entire economic mechanism. Let us not forget that capitalism itself, in essence, hinges on this: the ownership of machines. If these machines stop, ruin is immediate and absolute, as their substantial value, often acquired on credit in many major operations, exists solely in the context of permanent production.

But financial capital, with its characteristic fluidity, is linked to various sectors of industrial production, and this happens simultaneously through interconnections that make it highly susceptible to any crisis, no matter where it originates. The shares of one major company are funded by another, the credit and financial volume of one creates another somewhere else, and this entire fabric reaches savings and small capitals through banking institutions and the expansion of stock market speculation.

The economy of advanced capitalism—mechanized ownership and credit—sustains itself on a rigid unity, at the foundation of which lie extremely dangerous contradictions. Private economies, large and small enterprises, and personal wealth all rely on exceedingly fragile conditions.

At the culmination of the ideal of enrichment, this panorama unfolds: as men adopt it as their compass and embark on the journey toward personal gain in a liberal, individualistic manner, each with their own problems, economy, and dreams, a paradoxical consequence emerges. Suddenly, everyone becomes interconnected, susceptible to the same dangers, and playing the same hand. Paradoxically, the liberal-bourgeois mindset, which initiated an era of individualistic economic invigoration where everyone sought to forge his own wealth through free competition, ends up giving rise to a closed economic system. In this system, an intricately woven complexity binds all the riches of all individuals into a single organism.

## *Man Reclaims His "Social" Sense*

At the core of individualistic activity, and underpinning the described process of the capitalist system, there exists alongside a conscious overestimation of individual value a subconscious underestimation of the same. In a certain sense, man recognizes his vulnerability, his lack of secure connections, and finds himself exposed. Thus, the ideal of progressive enrichment could be seen as a human tendency to forge, through wealth, a kind of protection that would replace the social connections that were once evident before the individualistic era: connections based on shared faith, common guilds, cultural unity, uniform professions, the militia, and so forth.

It is becoming clear today that the individual dimension of man is almost exclusively tied to economic values, and that its historical cultivation, while inaugurating the capitalist era, has led us to the current state of the world, to great crises, to economic uncertainty for private fortunes, and above all, to vast masses in the most critical situation that can be conceived from a social and economic standpoint: that of the unemployed, the discarded, having absolutely nothing, with no possibility of gaining anything.

Thus, man has found that the securities, the protections he sought and once believed to be truly reliable, slip through his fingers. This leads him to a state of mind that inevitably drives him to discover and accept the perspectives of the "social." Perhaps it is of this nature that we can explain the worldwide prevalence of ways of life, institutions, and modes in which ideas of solidarity and common destiny currently prevail over any others. Thus, man forsakes his tendency to solely rely on individualistic categories and seeks and desires to enter with "others" in an order of more stable and secure accomplishments.

This phenomenon, of an increasingly intense assessment of "the social," is evident today in all manifestations that bear the typical stamp of the era. It also explains, for example, the reconnection of the great masses with the idea of the fatherland, finding in it both a refuge and an instrument, a mechanism through which only life itself can be possible. Furthermore, it explains the existence of numerous private economies of modest nature (wages, salaries, small distribution businesses), which acknowledge the impossibility of genuine enrichment, yet provide individuals with a balance, both moral and material, devoid of any socially resentful attitude. It also accounts for the homogenization of the masses (which we will examine later), the rediscovery of a sense of military morality, and the very essence of the youthful upheavals that are taking place.

### Unemployment: A Decisive Symptom

We have seen that industrial super-mechanization and the financial support of large companies demand, in the face of a looming crisis, the sacrifice of humans for machines. Rather than stopping the machines, which would result in the financial downfall of the industry, hundreds of thousands of men are thrown into forced unemployment if necessary. The ultimate and sole cause of this must be sought in the fact that the entire economic system responsible for industrial production has been based, from the very beginning, on the principle of progressive enrichment and free competition. That is to say, production's primary purpose is not to serve the needs of humans and provide them with consumer goods, but rather, something entirely different, completely disconnected from that purpose: to serve as a means of profit, a way to accumulate wealth.

The parasitic network surrounding the entire system of production and distribution has grown to enormous proportions. It is no longer just the industrialist or the entrepreneur who occupies a unique or even primary position within it. The intervention of financial capital, the presence of countless shareholders in public companies, speculation around industrial securities, intermediary commercial banks, and so forth, create a series of factors that weigh on and negatively influence the current super-capitalist economy.

The fact that the ultimate outcome of the entire system leads to unsustainable situations, arising from the fundamental contradictions that have been operating within it since its historical inception, seems to be evidence that is very difficult to deny today. This evidence is forced unemployment, the social reality that there are forty million people in the world without work and without bread. As we have discussed, it is clear that the most industrialized countries, where the capitalist system of overproduction reaches its highest achievements, suffer forced unemployment to a greater extent. In 1932, there were eleven and a half million unemployed in the United States, nearly three million in England, and five and a half million in Germany.

Now then, we do not find it logical or fair to condemn industrialization itself, and even less so the technical advances of mechanization. They belong to a realm of human values of great magnitude, and it is only the fact that they have been placed in the service of a misguided and erroneous concept of production that gives them an apparent disruptive and harmful character.

The forced unemployment that we observe today does not only affect or coincide with the most inept and worthless segments of the population. Among the millions of unemployed men, there are undoubtedly those with extensive professional qualifications and technical expertise in their respective industrial fields. Moreover, this issue does not exclusively concern wage earners or proletarians. Unemployment now threatens vast sections of the middle classes as well, and its severity is growing more acute among the youth with each passing day. The mindset of the unemployed man, or of someone at risk of becoming unemployed in the near future, bears a very unique tragic nature. It is possible that within this mindset, one of the most influential factors shaping the subversive outcomes of this era is taking shape.

It follows, then, that a radical shift has taken place in what we can term "social struggles." Up until now, during the ascendant period of capitalism, the working masses fought for the benefits that were obtained, achieving social improvements and wage increases. The slogan was to liberate workers from exploitation. It appears that all of this is undergoing a complete change, firstly, because there is the clear existence of a deep crisis, which renders the benefits of business enterprises problematic or non-existent in many cases, and if such benefits do not exist, then they can hardly be disputed by workers or anyone else. Moreover, wage increases obtained through inflationary and artificial measures, intended to trigger a rise in prices and a fictitious increase in the purchasing power of the masses, do not provide any real advantage. Secondly, it is not authentic exploitation that the proletarians ultimately suffer, but something worse or better, yet different: they are unemployed. In other words, they are reduced to a new social category, put in a dramatic situation of being residual beings, surplus, without anything to do.

All of these symptoms, therefore, indicate that we find ourselves at a crucial hour in the world. It will be difficult, within the current system, to find any solution that leads to a lasting resolution. The phenomenon of forced unemployment, we repeat, is helping to provide our era with an important element for the development of economic and political forms of life, the nature of which is not yet fully predictable. The point is for man to discover new tasks for man—new services. How and by what means these tasks will be discovered is not yet known with certainty. However, it *is* certain that they are one of the goals, one of the purposes pursued in the transmutative period currently in place.

### 8. The Uniformity of the Masses: The Political Uniform and its Authenticity

The presence of the youth in the core of political struggles has coincided with a noticeable phenomenon: the increase in the external display of the political affiliation they are associated with. This development has occurred at a time ripe for uniformity, a time of rediscovery of the social dimension of humanity—that is, a time of subordination and discipline to values and categories that are beyond the individual and collective.

### The Meaning of Uniformity

Evidently, throughout the period of liberal-bourgeois civilization, there has been a tendency to remove life from all uniformity. The cult of individual values logically led to the worship of dispersion, variety, and indiscipline. Such a cult manifested itself both in the political realm and in daily life, as well as in the appreciation or character of tastes. Among the things that were objects of aversion was, for example, the uniform, that is, unique and identical attire. Perhaps one can find in this fact the permanent hostility that groups and ideas more characteristic of the democratic-bourgeois spirit have had toward the military and soldiers, values inseparable from a concept of uniformity, and individuals who did not lose their character as "uniformed," representing both their function and its public outward expression.

During the democratic-bourgeois era, the uniform has been hated, and a profound underestimation has been directed toward it. But there is a unique aspect to this phenomenon, revealing how the bourgeois spirit follows criteria of refined affectation in its valuations. It turns out that the uniform has been disregarded, and it has always been seen as having a specific tendency, without being judged or understood in its true sense. Wearing a uniform was an aspiration for the bourgeoisie to stand out, to strengthen themselves, that is, to further assert individual personality. Nothing could be more mistaken or false. In reality, the opposite occurs. Those who put on a uniform are actually diminishing themselves as individuals, entering ranks where their individuality loses prominence and significance, and they become an anonymous number within those ranks.

It is not the uniform clothing, but rather the other one, the democratic-bourgeois attire, that actually fulfills and embodies the tendency to stand out and be valued individually. It can be said that what distinguishes the bourgeoisie is the eagerness to be distinguished. Therefore, their attire allows for an infinite variety of forms and resources through which social differentiation can be achieved. From the hat to the shoes, all the garments can be made of one fabric or another, of one color or another, and they can be adorned with numerous accessories, which give more or less elegance and prominence—that is, more or less significance to the individual.

Industrial mechanization and its consequence—that is, the mass production of identical objects—is one of the phenomena that began to engulf the very spirit and style from which they originated. Just as the super-capitalist economy has led to the near monopolization of once-distinct economies, even though it emerged from a period of liberal, individual economy, similarly, mass production has come to destroy the initial tendency toward diverse clothing.

## The Emergence of the Masses

The concept, now so common and widely used, of "the masses" is related to a very recent phenomenon, and perhaps many use it incorrectly. But the truth is, without a clear understanding of what the masses are, little can be truly comprehended about everything that has been unfolding for the past fifteen or twenty years, as it is the masses themselves who are carrying it out, executing it, and giving it meaning.

During the nineteenth century, a period that was distinctly individualistic and bourgeois, there were no masses. The emergence of masses as such, I repeat, is a recent phenomenon, arising in the very era in which we are currently living. Therefore, it is something that came after the period of liberal democratic dominance and the upward trajectory of capitalism, or at least coincided with its culmination and the inauguration or opening of its decline. Indeed, the individualistic civilization and the social and political forms it gave rise to were not conducive to the existence of masses. Masses are not mere agglomerations; they do not necessarily emerge alongside the presence of crowds. The political and social concept of the masses does not, in short, have much to do with the concept of majorities or minorities, which was characteristic of the era—now surpassed—that we have alluded to.

For crowds, aggregations, and large groups of people to fit into the concept of masses as they exist and act, certain characteristics must be present. For example, there needs to be a collective consciousness that is stronger in expression than the individual consciousness of those who make up the masses. Masses are homogeneous, and one becomes a part of them by possessing an essential connection with others, by renouncing and subordinating one's own being to the collective being that informs them. Masses are totalitarian, exclusive—in other words, they possess an awareness of being a complete, closed unity. The significance of masses is entirely disconnected from their numerical quantity, from the few or many individuals who comprise them.

Undoubtedly, there are other defining characteristics, and undoubtedly the concept of masses can be studied from characteristics different from the ones we have highlighted. However, these characteristics are real and exact, and they help us clarify the theme of this chapter.

At first glance, it can be perceived that the masses are something entirely foreign to the democratic-bourgeois mentality, and their existence cannot in any way predominate as long as the latter maintains its normal vigor. So then it is not the masses, but the parties, the groups, with their attachment to the concepts of majorities and minorities—that is, with their dependence on numerical evaluations, which of course are formed by a sum of "individuals," who add and add up to that, being individuals.

So then, far from being primarily about numerical quantity, although that is also naturally a factor, the masses can and do achieve predominance due to another set of qualities: their agility, their compactness, and their uniformity, their internal discipline. The phenomena we have studied in this digression—Bolshevism, Fascism, German socialist racism—are clear and formidable examples of the intervention and presence of the masses.

The masses are, by essence, bodies of a youthful nature, endowed with characteristics that are only found in young and new things. Let us not forget that the emergence of the masses coincides with a global era in which there is also a dominance and prevalence of "youth," and in which, as we

mentioned in the first digression, a messianic youth consciousness is at play.

## The Political Uniform

From the preceding lines, the conclusion is quite clear. The
introduction and utilization of uniforms, the external display
of unified and identical signs that is observed in the most recent world politics, is a logical outcome of being carried out by
the masses. Only the action of the masses leads to a "uniformed" political action, as we perceive it in almost all of Europe today.

The act of donning uniforms signifies the radical departure
from the democratic-bourgeois attitude and the emergence of
a different spirit. The integrating elements of the masses join
the ranks with a sense of sacrifice, while also feeling empow-
ered and invigorated through their commitment to the collective tasks that the masses undertake.

Not only in attire, but also in other traits that characterize
the action and presence of the masses, one can observe the
ease and swiftness with which their elements adopt the distinctive signs, greetings, and rites inherent to them, almost as
if by contagion, as if under the influence of an invisible and
fluid will.

It is evident that the Italian Fascists interpreted one of the
earliest manifestations of this phenomenon. Later, it has become generalized and widespread, not always merely as an
imitation, as many believe, but rather as a natural outgrowth
of something typical of the era, emerging alongside the actions that occur in this period. It also appears among the
class-conscious ranks of the proletariat. Notably, there is an
observation that highlights how such a style clashes with the
characteristics of the democratic-bourgeois spirit: among the
proletarians, those who are less inclined to align and identify
their struggles with the left-wing democratic-bourgeois

groups are the ones adopting uniformity, raising fists, and seeking the gestures and styles of militancy. In Spain, the socialist youth engaged in all these activities against the opinions and preferences of those within their party who opted for a moderate policy in line with the leftist bourgeoisie.

The uniformed political activity also demonstrates another aspect that contributes to clarifying one of its most distinct features: It is the value of sincerity and openness exhibited by its participants, the youthful character of dedication, without reservations or any calculation of cynicism or guile.

The uniformed political activist, who openly displays his character, provides the highest assurance that he is sincere and unlikely to deny his political flag, or abandon it for individual and dubious motives. Only the youth can indeed embrace such a political stance so naturally. On the contrary, the cautious and reserved attitude of the old members of democratic-bourgeois parties is well known.

When the youth enter the political arena, they incorporate the value of sincerity and present themselves as they truly are. The young person aligns himself with a flag, with ideals, and stands out by displaying them, enveloped in their essence. He believes that political and social ideas should be brought out into the open, to the surface, for all to see.

The mature sectors that witness the emergence of such a phenomenon react with dissenting judgments, displaying their classic wisdom by expressing that ideas—the ideal, as they put it with a touch of enchantment and pretense—should not be linked to a garment, a gesture, or anything of similar frivolity. Instead, they should be guarded deep within the chest, within the heart of a man, and enshrined there. However, this sentiment fails to move the youth, who have myriad practical reasons to know that those who keep their ideals hidden "deep within the heart" are often the ones who readily discard them, change their stance, and fluctuate from one side to the other, or act without recalling what they claim to treasure and revere so deeply.

The uniformed youth know, in the end, that it is precisely they—with the outward emblem that distinguishes them, having their ideas attached to their arm, their fist, their shirt, or their cap—who are truly committed with firmness and sincerity, permanence and sacrifice, to a cause. And therefore, they mockingly invite the mature and sensible people not to link ideas to organs as deep as the heart, but to bring them out into the open, so they can be seen, presenting them with simplicity, with the certainty that changing a shirt is harder than changing a heart (or a jacket).

# CONCLUSION

Indeed, thus is Europe, and that is the most accurate profile that Europe presents to us today. Naturally, we are also a part of it, and these phenomena will have their expression among us as well. Under our own skies, the Spanish contribution to the global transmutation will take shape. I do not know if it will happen sooner or later. However, what I am firmly convinced of is that we will arrive in time, and our voice will be heard.

Triumphant political manifestations have indeed emerged in Europe, as we have observed. Many claim that there are only two such manifestations—Fascism and Bolshevism—and that there are no other distinct alternatives. We do not accept this verdict as true. Those who hold this belief also suggest that the future will be a struggle between only these two banners, and that we are already within the midst of these conflicts. Once again, we express our dissenting opinion.

A global transformation is underway. Signs of it include Bolshevism, Italian Fascism, German socialist racism, and the styles and modes we have described in the preceding pages. These are eruptions, initiations, already imbued with what is to come, but they are by no means definitive, permanent, or conclusive. And certainly, both Bolshevism and Fascism, as well as racism, are national and restricted phenomena, lacking global scale or depth.

Perhaps the voice of Spain, the presence of Spain, when it is fully realized and achieved, will give the transmutative reality its most perfect and fertile meaning, the form that will brilliantly etch it into the pages of universal history.

ENJOYED THIS BOOK?

TO READ MORE, VISIT US AT

ANTELOPEHILLPUBLISHING.COM

www.ingramcontent.com/pod-product-compliance
Lightning Source LLC
Chambersburg PA
CBHW020402130626
46549CB00006B/2407